Everything's Negotiable

Everything's Negotiable

. . . When You Know How to Play the Game

Eric Wm. Skopec and Laree S. Kiely

American Management Association

New York • Atlanta • Boston • Chicago • Kansas City • San Francisco • Washington, D.C.
Brussels • Mexico City • Tokyo • Toronto

This publication is designed to provide accurate and authoritative
information in regard to the subject matter covered. It is sold with
the understanding that the publisher is not engaged in rendering
legal, accounting, or other professional service. If legal advice or
other expert assistance is required, the services of a competent
professional person should be sought.

Library of Congress Cataloging-in-Publication Data

Skopec, Eric W., 1946–
    Everything's negotiable—when you know how to play the game /
Eric Wm. Skopec and Laree S. Kiely.
        p.   cm.
    Includes bibliographical references and index.
    ISBN 0-8144-5161-6
    1. Negotiation in business.   I. Kiely, Laree.   II. Title.
HD58.6.S59   1994
658.4—dc20   93-47938
                                                                CIP

Printing number

10   9   8   7   6   5   4

Contents

Everything's Negotiable

Introduction

Welcome to *Everything's Negotiable . . . When You Know How to Play the Game*. You are about to learn a lot about negotiation, and you may even have some fun along the way. In the pages ahead, you will find:

- Step-by-step instructions showing you how to get what you want, at home and at work
- Expert recommendations on handling difficult people
- Specific information that will help you decide what you want and how to get it in many different kinds of negotiation

The principles and concepts listed here will help you sail through your negotiations. In addition, reading this book will give you:

- Practical advice from famous and skilled negotiators, advice that works as well in your negotiations as in theirs
- Summaries of the best current research so you can figure out what's going on around you and take charge
- Information about different countries and cultures so that you will be more effective in your negotiations
- Descriptions of common tricks and traps so you can stay on top of the game
- Examples of real-life blunders with object lessons so you avoid these mistakes in your own negotiations
- Cases you can use to test your own skills and compare your answers with those of the experts

That's a full agenda, so let's get down to business. By reading this introduction, you will see that negotiation is part of your daily life and that there is good reason to be concerned about it. And you will get a chance to preview the rest of the book.

Negotiation as Part of Your Daily Life

If you were to reconstruct a typical day, it might look a little like this:

7:00 A.M.   Breakfast with the family. Discussed buying grocer-
               ies, stopping at the dry cleaners, and driving the
               children to a school activity this evening.

8:00 A.M.   Meeting with the boss. Discussed three new proj-
               ects and set deadlines for two of them.

9:30 A.M.   Conducted performance review with subordinate.
               He has not fulfilled several obligations, and you
               put him on notice: Shape up or ship out.

10:45 A.M.   Returned telephone call from angry customer. A
               product has not satisfied her, and she wants you to
               repair or replace the unit.

11:30 A.M.   Lunch with a customer. She needs several units to
               replace older ones, but she is having difficulty with
               financing.

1:25 P.M.   Stopped to look at a new car. The dealer was
               anxious to make a deal and offered some very
               attractive options.

3:00 P.M.   Met with another member of your organization. He
               doesn't have enough parts to meet a critical deliv-
               ery schedule and would like to "borrow" some
               from one of your shipments.

3:45 P.M.   Called your son's teacher to schedule a parent-
               teacher conference.

4:00 P.M.   Conference call with other members of your church
               board. The budget for the new year is almost com-
               plete, but you need to cut a few hundred dollars
               from some special projects.

5:00 P.M.   Caught a cab to the airport for an overnight busi-
               ness trip. Cab fare was $15, to which you added a
               $3 tip.

7:00 P.M.   Arrived at your destination, took the shuttle to
               your hotel, and checked in. Because your company
               made a reservation for you, you paid the corporate
               rate of $85 instead of the regular $120.

Even if your day doesn't seem that tightly scheduled, you can list similar activities. And even this list probably leaves out countless other dealings with people. Many are so routine that you forget all about them—for example, buying a newspaper, grabbing a quick sandwich in the afternoon, talking with some friends, and stopping for a drink after checking in to the hotel.

"Life is negotiation."

Danny Devito, *Playboy* (February 1993): 60.

Would you agree with us that each one of these dealings was a negotiation? Some are pretty clear. For example, almost everyone would agree that both of your customer contacts were negotiations. Both customers wanted you to do something, and you made deals that satisfied them. The car dealer offered to sell you a car with lots of options, but you said no because you figured you could do better elsewhere. What about the conference call with the other church board members? As a group, you needed to make a decision, and you did your best to satisfy everyone.

Those are all pretty good examples of negotiation. What about your other contacts with people during the day? Let's start with the family breakfast. Someone needs to pick up groceries, get the dry cleaning, and drive the children to school. You got off the hook because you would be out of town.

The meeting with your boss wasn't much of a negotiation if you said yes to everything he assigned you. However, there was lots of negotiation if you said yes and asked for something in return. The same is true of your meetings with your subordinate and the other manager at work. If there was no disagreement, you probably wouldn't consider these meetings as negotiations. However, if someone said "yes, but" or "no, because," it was pretty clear that you were involved in a negotiation. In other words, you decided whether you were in a negotiation. If you just went along with the other person, it probably wasn't much of a negotiation. If you tried to add conditions or make changes in the deal, you would probably call the meetings negotiations.

Does the same hold true for your other dealings during the day? We think so. Arranging the parent-teacher conference may have been easy, but if the teacher had wanted to schedule it for a time that was inconvenient for you, the conversation could have quickly turned into a negotiation.

The cab fare to the airport was posted on the meter, and you didn't argue. In many other countries, though, passengers are expected to negotiate fares before the ride. Failing to do so is a sure sign of a tourist, and you may very well get taken.

The hotel gave you a corporate rate—a pretty good deal compared to the posted rate. But you might have gotten an even better deal if you had asked for it. The real cost of opening a room at many first-class hotels is about $30, and most hotels are willing to deal if it doesn't look as if they will fill up for the evening. Hotel management is under pressure to deal for two reasons: Keeping you happy will increase the chance you will return, and they don't make any money on rooms that are vacant.

Many of your other dealings represented opportunities for negotiation that you overlooked or chose to ignore. Think about them, and ask yourself, "Could I have gotten a better deal?" If you answer yes, you missed an opportunity to negotiate.

Here's what we want you to see: Every time you deal with another person, you have an opportunity to negotiate to improve your situation. You probably grab at some of these chances, let others pass, and don't even notice some opportunities. But in every case, you have a chance to negotiate, and you alone decide whether you try.

Good Reasons to Be Concerned About Negotiation

You already see the best reason to be concerned about negotiation. Just about everything you do involves working with other people. Every time you deal with another person, you have a chance to make things better—for yourself and the other party—through negotiation. At the same time, lots of other people are looking for opportunities to deal with you. Some of them are ethical and trustworthy, others are not. You alone decide whether to deal with them, and you alone are accountable for the results.

What's more, basic changes in our society have increased opportunities for negotiation—for example:

▪ *There are far more people for you to negotiate with.* Size is one of the most noticeable changes. Our population is growing about 1 percent a year and passed 250 million around 1990. Many of these people cluster together in large metropolitan areas, and nearly half live in cities with populations of 1 million or more.

- *You have to deal with people from many cultures and countries.* The composition of society is changing as it grows. Studies tell us that the United States will be a far different country by the year 2000. We can already see its new outlines.

More than 40 percent of our recent population growth has come from immigration. When our citizens talk about home, they name countries from A to Z—literally, Afghanistan to Zimbabwe. Here are three statistics that make this point particularly memorable:

1. One person out of five walking down the street in any major city was probably born outside the United States.
2. School districts in major cities like Los Angeles teach basic courses in more than 100 languages.
3. The last census required more than 630 distinct ethnic codes for recording data.

The numbers would be even more impressive if we added tourists, visiting businesspeople, and illegal immigrants. Here's what you need to remember: Day in and day out, you deal with people who look at the world in new and interesting ways. Many come from cultures where bartering is a way of life and negotiation is second nature to them.

 **GOOD TO KNOW**

The growing number of foreign-born professionals in the United States is changing our working lives. Conservative estimates indicate that more than 25,000 Americans work for Japanese managers on temporary assignment in this country.

- *There is great economic pressure for you to be a skilled negotiator.* The United States is struggling to escape one of the worst recessions on record. Signs of trouble are all around us: Businesses are laying off workers, "rightsizing," or closing up shop; unemployment is rising; poverty and homelessness are reaching record levels; our national income growth is barely measurable.

Like most economists, we believe that the recession will be over soon. We also know that it will have a lasting effect on the way people think about the world. We are getting used to a society where there isn't enough to go around. People do not count on a better tomorrow and are learning to get their share before someone else does. Some have even learned to think that anything goes as long as they get what they want.

We aren't advocating cutthroat competition, but you can be sure that some of the people around you are watching out for number one. Developing your own negotiation skills may be the only way to hold your own.

- *New business arrangements are changing the way we deal with people at work.* Take a broad-brush look at our history. We began as a nation of farmers and became a nation of manufacturers sometime around World War II. Today, technology is making us a nation of information workers. With the growth of information-intensive work, the way we do things and the things we value are changing dramatically. Skilled workers no longer need unions to protect them; they cut their own deals, often working as consultants or independent contractors. And fewer and fewer companies rely on traditional bid-price purchasing. They establish stable partnerships with customers and suppliers, sharing information networks and working on a just-in-time basis. We could add to the list, but you see the point: With the changing nature of work, the strength of your negotiating skills is likely to determine how well you get along.

- *You receive countless proposed deals every day.* As our society has become more complex, the number of proposals brought to us every day has mushroomed. Day in and day out, we are bombarded with proposals. At work, outside vendors and other members of our own organizations bring deals to our attention. You can choose from new job assignments, educational or training opportunities, benefits packages, consulting programs, and investment opportunities.

The barrage doesn't stop when you get home. Turn on the TV or pick up a magazine, and you are deluged with proposals. Paid programs promise instant fortunes by dealing in real estate, explain the latest "investment secrets," and promote "unlimited personal power." Some are little more than get-rich-quick schemes, but others may have value to you.

Just sorting out the proposals could be a full-time job. Identifying those that are worth pursuing and making the opportunities work for you call for top-notch negotiation skills.

What's Ahead in This Book

We titled this book *Everything's Negotiable . . . When You Know How to Play the Game* because negotiation has a lot in common with some games. Both games and negotiation:

- Have rules, but the rules in both can be changed at will.
- Require two or more players.
- Have definite goals or objectives.
- Require players to combine strategy and tactics.
- Require specific skills to play effectively.
- May generate fears that keep you from doing your best.
- Can be a source of fun and profit if you play well.

This book will help you develop the skills and knowledge you need to overcome your fears and play your best. Notice that the text is organized like instructions for most games. Beginning with the object of the game and moving on to discuss the skills you need, the instructions tell you how to set up the game, explain how to play a basic game, and introduce strategy and tactics. Finally, the instructions mention etiquette and conclude with instructions for advanced games.

Chapter 1 starts with the object of the game. This is where we define negotiation and ask you to think about what you have to win or lose. You may be surprised to learn that sometimes you should not negotiate. It's also important to know that win-win solutions are not always best. Finding them takes lots of time and energy, and they may not get you what you want.

Chapter 2 explains what you need to win the game—not dice or plastic guns but the fundamental skills you need to be a blue-chip negotiator. There is nothing mysterious about these skills. We show you what they are, how to recognize them in yourself and in others, how to cope with your own shortcomings, and how to cope with the strengths and weaknesses of other players.

Chapter 3 discusses the order of play. You will learn how to conduct any negotiation using the Relate-Explore-Propose-Agree cycle, and we walk you through each of the steps. By the time you finish this chapter, you will know when to talk and when to listen, how to get critical information from other players, how to make offers, and how to respond to offers from the other person. You will know as well how to close a deal and get agreement in writing so you have something useful to carry away with you.

Chapter 4 introduces you to pregame planning. Once the season begins, you need to focus on specific situations, and this chapter provides everything you need: an overview of the negotiation process emphasizing the critical elements for which you must prepare, a worksheet with specific questions to help you prepare for any encounter, guides for turning your preparation into specific actions and questions for each step of the negotiation process, and some tips for controlling anxiety that might limit your effectiveness.

Chapter 5 introduces special strategies and tactics. They make it possible for you to decide what you want and how you can get it in just about every situation. If you are worried about the other players—the people with whom you negotiate—wait until you get to Chapter 6 on etiquette. Here we explain how to deal with people from other cultures and how to deal with the "bad guys," people who push others around, and what you can do to protect yourself. By the time you finish this chapter, you will be able to work with people from a variety of cultures and counter the ten most common moves the bad guys use.

Chapters 7 through 10 introduce some advanced games—special situations where negotiation is particularly important. We show you how to use what you've already learned to manage the negotiations that have the greatest effect on your daily life. Chapter 7 focuses on the skills in buying and selling. You will see that the same skills you use every day to get good deals on personal items can help you in major corporate negotiations.

Chapter 8 shows you how to use negotiation skills to build and maintain relationships in professional situations. Colleagues, clients, customers, and coworkers all present opportunities for negotiation, and we'll show you how to manage relationships with each.

Chapter 9 shows you how to use your negotiation skills to handle some sticky situations at work: getting support from your colleagues; negotiating organizational changes; obtaining additional resources, such as a raise; and negotiating a smooth termination.

Finally, Chapter 10 introduces you to the world of the mediator. We show you how to use your skills to help the people around you solve their special problems. You will learn to recognize spots you should avoid and how to get out of them gracefully. You will even learn how to get other people to negotiate with one another in serious, responsible ways.

 **GOOD TO KNOW**

Good to Know sections are found throughout this book. They give you a chance to look at some useful information, and remember key concepts. Some tell stories that are fun to read and worth remembering.

Each chapter closes with a Your Move case or two that gives you a chance to test your skills by applying them to common problems. Try solving the problem on your own before you look ahead to the Analysis that follows each Your Move section.

While you're reading, watch for the following elements designed to make learning fun and interesting.

Quotations present useful advice from skilled negotiators. Some quotations come from well-known figures; others come from people who have worked in relative obscurity. But all are skilled negotiators, and all have something important to say about negotiation.

Everyone screws up from time to time, and we've used *Object Lessons* to highlight some critical blunders in negotiation. They're fun reading, and we've concluded each story with an object lesson that may help you avoid making the same mistake.

Finally, *Good to Know* sections present bits and pieces of information that may help you in dealing with particular situations. For example, did you know that 40 percent of employees in the United States don't believe anything management says or that Chinese negotiators value detailed information and ask many questions to make sure they have all the facts before making a decision? These bits of information may not matter to everyone, but they can make a difference when you are negotiating with an angry employee or trying to make a deal with someone from the People's Republic of China.

There's a lot ahead of you. Read it for fun, read it for profit, and reread it whenever you are getting ready for an important negotiation.

1

The Object of the Game

Negotiation is like any other game: To play it well, you need to know what you want and how to get it. The "how" will occupy the rest of the book; in this chapter, you will learn to establish the "what." Here's what you will able to do when you finish this chapter:

- Recognize opportunities that might otherwise slip by.
- Set objectives that shape your approach to negotiation in positive, productive ways.
- Practice win-win negotiation when appropriate, and other approaches when they give you a better chance of getting what you want.
- Walk away from negotiations you can't win.

Recognizing Opportunities for Negotiation

You have an opportunity to negotiate every time you deal with another person. Every time you ask someone to do something for you, every time someone asks you to do something for him or her, every time you need to make plans that involve someone else, you have an opportunity to negotiate. We really mean it. Every time!

We are constantly surprised by the opportunities most people miss. They range from small opportunities (buying groceries) to big

 GOOD TO KNOW

Negotiation is a shared decision involving two or more parties concerning the resolution of a conflict, often about the allocation of scarce resources.

opportunities (when the boss asks them to undertake a new project). We have often wondered why people miss these opportunities. Our answer will help you recognize opportunities that others overlook.

Some Common Traps

People overlook opportunities to negotiate because they fall prey to four common traps. Knowing that these traps exist will help you avoid them and capitalize on the opportunities that are all around you.

First, people miss opportunities to negotiate because they don't pay attention. It's as if they were on autopilot, sleepwalking through their days without noticing anything going on around them. Here's how to check if you're on autopilot. Make a list of the people you talk to in any twenty-four-hour period. That may sound like an easy task, but studies show that the number of people is far larger than you may realize. Whether you are sitting in your office, walking down the street, or driving to work, you come into contact with hundreds of people every day, every one of whom provides an opportunity to negotiate.

Second, people miss opportunities to negotiate because the news media mislead us by focusing on big deals, the once-in-a-lifetime negotiations. For example, magazines recently have included stories about the North American Free Trade Agreement, a foreign company's efforts to buy an American airline, the end of a strike costing the company $5 million a day, and bond holders' opposition to a corporate restructuring. Of course, these negotiations are clearly newsworthy. But they are only a few of the negotiations that take place every day. And here's what's really important to remember: The best way to get ready for the big deals, the once-in-a-lifetime opportunities, is to practice the skills you need every day.

The third reason people miss opportunities to negotiate is that they think the cards are stacked against them. They think they don't have a chance in the negotiation and don't even try.

We understand the feeling. We won't tell you how many times we have been on the short end. However, we will tell you that the worse things seem, the more reason you have to negotiate. Negotiation isn't likely to hurt you, and there is always a chance that it will make the situation better. It doesn't cost anything to refuse the first offer, and the second may be sweeter.

Why would someone negotiate with you when they hold all the cards? Simple: If they are smart, they know that few things are ever settled. If they force you to accept something you don't like, you will look for ways to settle the score. At the same time, you should remember that it's wise to negotiate even when you hold all of the cards. Negotiation will reduce resentment and promote a stable agreement.

Finally, some people miss opportunities because they are afraid to try. For example, when you buy something, it's a lot less embarrassing to pay the posted price than ask for a better deal. It's a lot less fun, too. We talk about fear in Chapter 4. For now, remember that it doesn't hurt to try. The other person can always say no, and you haven't lost anything by trying.

Setting Your Objectives

Faced with all these opportunities to negotiate, how do you decide which to pursue and which to ignore? And how do you decide what you want out of each? Knowing what you want, who can give it to you, and how hard you are willing to work for it is the key to choosing your spots. The important thing is to make sure you are looking at the full picture; that means understanding the substantive issues, your relationship to the other players, and the amount of effort you plan to invest in the negotiation process.

The Substantive Issues

Substantive issues are the stuff or content of negotiation. You wouldn't negotiate if you didn't think you had something to gain, and the substantive issues are the things you are trying to get.

Substantive issues are relatively simple in some negotiations. When you set out to buy a car, you probably know what you want and how much you are prepared to spend. Price is the key issue. As you dicker with the sales agent, several related issues may come into play. The sticker price is the starting point; your discussions can include rebates, trade-in value, paint and accessories, and so on. We could list lots of extras, but you already know what matters most: the bottom line, the amount of money out of your pocket to buy the car.

Substantive issues can also be complex. Think about your concerns in accepting a new job. Salary may be a major point, but there are several other considerations. Some are directly related to compensation; medical benefits and retirement programs come to mind. Other considerations are not directly linked to pay: work schedules, location, protection from layoffs, and the amount of travel required. And what about training opportunities? They may be related to compensation, but they also have other implications.

The number of issues involved complicates negotiation. Sometimes you can trade one against another—more travel in exchange for a preferred home base—but sometimes you need to hold your ground on all of them.

Negotiations become even more complex when labor and management have a range of issues on the table, when companies battle over merger agreements, and when nations try to settle long-standing trade or border disputes. Dealing with complex situations requires extensive knowledge of the situation and alternatives. However, these are still substantive issues, the first of the three things you need to consider.

The Other Players

Your relationship with the other players is the second item to consider in setting your objectives. Relationships influence and are influenced by negotiations. The way you negotiate should depend on how you

 **OBJECT LESSON**

Balancing substantive issues and relationships is often very difficult, and not all companies do it well.

Facing a difficult economic situation, a major defense contractor pressured its employees to accept substantial cuts in wages and benefits. The employees had few alternatives, and their union eventually agreed.

The company got a favorable contract, but it paid a large price. Employee resentment reduced productivity and eventually led to sabotage. Government inspectors examining one of the company's products found forty-five pounds of trash—hamburger wrappers, Styrofoam cups, broken tools, and even a typewriter—concealed in sensitive control areas. The entire unit had to be rebuilt and special inspection procedures added for all products. In the end, the company incurred costs that far exceeded their savings on wages and benefits.

The lesson: Don't overlook relationships when you push your
position.

feel about the other party, and your feelings will change as the result of each negotiation.

Some relationships don't matter very much; at least they don't to most people. For example, you probably don't lose much sleep thinking about your relationship to the salesperson when you set out to buy a car. You don't care what she thinks of you, and you can negotiate as if it didn't matter.

Other relationshps are more valuable. For example, relationships should be a major concern when negotiating for a new job. You probably want to get as much as you can, but you need to be careful to avoid offending your new boss. At the same time, many potential bosses would like to get you as cheaply as possible, but they shouldn't beat you down so much that they get an unmotivated, demoralized employee.

Transaction Costs

The amount of time and effort you are willing to invest in the negotiation process is the third factor to consider. These are the direct costs of being involved in negotiation. They are overlooked more often than the other two factors, and people often pay a high price for failing to consider them.

The 1991 Nobel Prize in economics was awarded to Ronald Coase, a retired professor at the University of Chicago, for his work describing transaction costs. In its simplest form, Coase's work pointed out that the value of any agreement is reduced by the amount of time and effort invested in reaching it.

An example will show exactly what we mean. A friend planning to buy a new car decided to do it right. He began by reading *The Car Buyer's Art*. Filled with ideas, he did extensive research on current

---

Golda Meir, Prime Minister of Israel during a particularly turbulent period (1969–1974), insisted on face-to-face meetings while negotiating with the Arabs. A journalist questioned the need for these meetings; "Even divorces are arranged without personal confrontation," he said. "I'm not interested in a divorce," Mrs. Meir replied. "I'm interested in a marriage."

From *The Little, Brown Book of Anecdotes* (Boston: Little, Brown, 1985), p. 394.

---

prices, sales figures, rebates, estimated repair costs, finance rates, and just about everything else he could think of. Armed with this information, he visited more than two dozen local dealers to see who was hungriest. Once he had selected a dealer, he asked a relatively young, inexperienced salesperson to take him for a test drive. Then he submitted an offer, one that was so far below market there was no chance that it would be accepted. That was part of his plan. Over the next month, he returned to the dealership several times, never wavering from his initial offer. Eventually the salesperson offered a compromise. Our friend greedily accepted, and the deal was closed. He did a great deal of bragging until he met a neighbor who had bought the same make and model. Doing no advance work, she had just stopped by the dealer, made what she thought was a reasonable offer, and bought an identical car for barely $500 more.

By our calculations, our friend's efforts had saved him less than three dollars an hour. That's not a very good deal when you think how he could have used this time. He earns far more at work, and time with family and friends is certainly more rewarding.

Transaction costs are the value of your time and effort committed to making the deal. They include the cost of your time, the cost of the other party's time, and the costs of anyone else involved in the deal. And, as the wag says, God help you if lawyers get involved.

Should You Always Try to Win?

Over the last several years, teachers, consultants, and writers have said a lot about win-win negotiation. Win-win means different things to different people, but the key idea is that each of the parties involved gets something of value to them. This is a relatively new approach to negotiation, and a little history will put it in perspective.

Until a few years ago, many professionals thought negotiation was always a competitive activity. They looked at each negotiation as an opportunity to get what they wanted, no matter how it affected the other party. Books and popular seminars often taught the same approach. *Getting to Yes*, published in 1981, made the first credible case for win-win negotiation.

The emphasis on win-win negotiation is a healthy antidote to earlier, shortsighted thinking. Many businesses have benefited from the new approach because win-win agreements make good business sense. They promote stable agreements because neither party is trying to recover something lost in the previous round of negotiation.

OBJECT LESSON

Donald Petersen, former CEO of Ford Motor Company, provides a great example of a win-win agreement. Both Ford and its suppliers were unhappy with the paperwork required to pay some invoices. Payment took an average of seven months when there were discrepancies because neither side trusted the other. Gathering a team to solve the problem, Ford and its suppliers overcame communication barriers and a confrontational relationship. As a result, Petersen explains, "Team members agreed to share more information up front and to arrive at a cost analysis system that was mutually acceptable. The time required to settle a bill dropped from 220 days to 22 days, and the number of steps in the process from 87 to 43."

The lesson: Both sides can win when they set their minds to it.

From Donald E. Petersen and John Hillkirk, *A Better Idea* (Boston: Houghton Mifflin, 1991), pp. 256–257.

Win-win agreements also provide a foundation for further dealings. Good faith demonstrated in one negotiation naturally paves the way for future dealings. And win-win agreements also make it easy to smooth out business problems for everyone's benefit.

There is a lot to be said for win-win bargaining, and we believe you should practice it whenever possible. But in lots of cases, you may not be able to pursue a win-win solution. The time, the place, and/or the parties may make it impractical to work for a win-win agreement. Take a careful look at Exhibit 1-1. Here is your full range of options: win-win, win-lose, lose-win, and lose-lose.

With all these alternatives, does it ever make sense to lose? Answering that question is complicated by our language. *Lose* has meanings that get in the way of objective thinking. Once you get past the emotional response, it's easy to recognize some cases where you may well want to lose.

When Losing Is Your Best Bet

1. *You don't care what happens.* The issue doesn't matter much to you, and winning would take more effort than it's worth. Remember what we said about transaction costs? Whenever winning will cost

Exhibit 1-1.   Bargaining options.

Your Objective

		Win	Lose
The Other Party's Objective	Win	Both parties win.	You lose and the other party wins.
	Lose	You win and the other party loses.	Both parties lose.

more than the prize is worth, losing makes sense. There are also some circumstances when you need to think about far more than economic costs. Dealing with unpleasant people, working in uncomfortable settings, and frequent travel are all transactions costs to consider in weighing the value of the prize.

2. *Time is against you.* When deadlines loom, it makes sense to be done with an issue rather than taking time to find a winning solution. Crafting win-win agreements can take a lot of time. Winning at the other player's expense may take even more time, especially if the other party refuses to give up. So if you are facing a deadline, losing makes sense because it is the easiest way to close a negotiation and get on to other business.

3. *You have bigger fish to fry.* You could win a particular negotiation, but you can get greater benefits by losing. Consider the case of a merchant dealing with an angry customer who would like to return a broken small appliance shortly after its warranty has expired. The merchant is clearly within her rights in refusing to accept the return, but losing this negotiation could make far more sense, especially if the customer is a loyal customer who may bring more business in the future. Here it makes sense to lose the negotiation as a way of protecting a valued relationship and building business for the future.

OBJECT LESSON

Even major corporations find it makes sense to give in sometimes. Consider the problem Disney faced in trying to meet the April 12, 1992, opening date for its $5 billion theme park near Paris. Construction contractors demanded payment for "extra" work totaling nearly $150 million. Euro Disney's CEO initially called the demands blackmail and refused to pay. However, the builders won the support of the French press and threatened to picket the grand opening. Realizing it was in a no-win situation, Disney paid off forty of the most vigorous protesters and opened negotiations with the others.

The lesson: Never be afraid to lose when you have bigger fish to fry.

From Bill Echikson, "Disney's Rough Ride in France," *Fortune* (March 23, 1992): 14, 18.

Making Up Your Own Mind

Plan to lose some of the time. But be on your guard. Some negotiators will do everything they can to make you want to lose. They will manipulate the situation to make it look as if you have nothing to gain by winning. They will go out of their way to delay the negotiation if they know you are facing a deadline. And they will try to create the impression that you have bigger fish to fry. These are all time-honored strategies. (In Chapter 5, you will learn how to protect yourself from these gambits.) Recognize that you should use your own judgment. Set your own objectives, and make your own plans. Test your own judgment on the three cases set out at the end of this chapter and then compare your analysis to ours. You can set your objectives by asking three questions:

1. *Is the substantive issue important to you?* This can be a difficult question, especially when you are inclined to say "sort of" or "compared to what?" Try rephrasing the question: Do you stand to gain more than the probable transactions costs? If you think so, say yes; the issue is important to you. If you stand to gain less than the probable transaction costs, say no; the issue isn't important to you. Now take a look at Exhibit 1-2. It looks like Exhibit 1-1, but we've

Exhibit 1-2. Bargaining options when substantive issues are important.

Your Objective

	Win	Lose
Win	Both parties win	You lose and the other party wins.
Lose	You win and the other party loses.	Both parties lose.

The Other Party's Objective

shaded one column. If the substantive issue is important to you, find a solution in the left column, the shaded side. If the substantive issue isn't important to you, look to the right side, the unshaded side.

2. *Do you value your relationship with the other party?* If your answer is yes, pick a solution where the other party wins, one in the shaded portion of Exhibit 1-3. If your answer is no, it's okay for the other side to lose. Look to the bottom of the table, the unshaded portion.

Now you can see when it makes sense to look for a win-win solution. Aim for a win-win solution when the substantive issue is important to you, and you value your relationship with the other side. Exhibit 1-4 shows how your analysis leads to this conclusion.

3. *Is time an important factor?* We're interested only in deadlines here; we've already factored in transition costs. If you aren't facing a deadline, say no; time is not important. Stick with your strategy based on answers to the first two questions. On the other hand, if you are facing a deadline, time is important. Plan to stick with your original strategy for a while, and then back off to a losing strategy that will let you finish quickly when the deadline gets closer. We'll say more about getting out of losing situations at the end of this chapter.

Exhibit 1-3. Bargaining options when the relationship is important.

The Other Party's Objective		Your Objective: Win	Your Objective: Lose
	Win	Both parties win.	You lose and the other party wins.
	Lose	You win and the other party loses.	Both parties lose.

Exhibit 1-4. Bargaining options when both substantive issues and the relationship are important.

The Other Party's Objective		Your Objective: Win	Your Objective: Lose
	Win	Both parties win.	You lose and the other party wins.
	Lose	You win and the other party loses.	Both parties lose.

Exhibit 1-5 shows how we would apply this method to the Your Move cases at the end of this chapter. Don't feel discouraged if your answers don't agree with ours; we expect you to use your own judgment. After all, you are a mature professional, too. The value of our method is in making sure you consider the key factors we've described: substantive issues, relationships, and time.

To help you exercise your judgment, look at Exhibit 1-5.

Exhibit 1-5.   Factors to think about before choosing a negotiating strategy.

Strategy	Necessary Conditions
Win-win	• The issue is important to you, and • You value your relationship with the other party, and • You have enough time to search for an approach that satisfies all parties' objectives.
Win-lose	• The issue is important to you, but • Preserving your relationship with the other party doesn't matter, and • You have the time to beat the other party down. • Or, you would like to find a win-win solution but know the other party will try to take advantage of you. Working for a win-lose solution is your only chance to break even.
Lose-win	• The issue isn't important to you, but • You value your relationship with the other party and think letting her win will help build a lasting relationship. • Or, you are under time pressure and are willing to accept a lose-win solution because it is the fastest way to be done.
Lose-lose	• The issue is relatively unimportant to both parties. • You may build a relationship based on mutual suffering, but it is not a major concern. Time and/or transaction costs are primary considerations; parties accept lose-lose solutions because they are often the fast way of resolving an issue.

Walking Away From a Losing Negotiation

By now you see that there are some negotiations in which you don't want to be involved. These are the negotiations you would willingly lose. Your life would be much better if you could avoid these negotiations altogether. A really clever person would never let one of these negotiations get started.

Unfortunately, you can't always avoid the losers. Sometimes you get involved before you realize that a negotiation is going to be a loser. And sometimes someone else drags you into a negotiation that you would rather avoid. How do you get out of a loser quickly and gracefully?

Most of us would just like to say something like, "Thank you kindly; do what you will," and walk away, trusting the other party to handle matters in a reasonable way. Unfortunately, you can't always count on the other party to do the right thing. And even if the other person did handle things in a just and equitable way, there is good reason to avoid such an approach.

Recent research has identified a phenomenon known as the winner's curse. You may not have heard the name before, but there is a good chance you have experienced the feeling. Put yourself in the following spot: You have been looking for a good used car. You know what kind of a car you want and about what you should pay. After shopping around, you find one advertised in the paper. You call the owner and arrange to inspect the car. You find it to be well maintained and in good condition. And the price, $8,500, is just about right. However, you want to see if you can get a better deal so you try a low-ball offer, $5,000. Surprisingly, the owner doesn't even flinch. Without missing a beat, she shakes your hand, smiles, and says, "Good, we have a deal." How do you feel?

We've used this problem in countless seminars. Almost without exception, people react in two steps: first, "What's wrong?" or "What did I miss?" followed by, "I could have done better!" Those feelings are the winner's curse. We joke about these reactions in our seminars, but you never want the other party to get this feeling. Why? Because these feelings can undo everything you were trying to accomplish by losing.

If you were trying to get out of a negotiation because you knew you couldn't win, you've just told the other party that he could have gotten more. Remember the schoolyard bully who took any sign of weakness as an invitation for further attack. Aggressive negotiators respond the same way, and you face a future of being drawn into losing negotiations until you get tough.

Even more important, if you were willing to lose a negotiation because you wanted to build a relationship, giving in too soon sends the wrong message. The other party won't place much value on what you've given her. She may even doubt your goodwill.

GOOD TO KNOW

Almost everyone, even high-level corporate officials, can fall prey to the winner's curse. Working with M.B.A. candidates, corporate CEOs, certified public accountants, and investment bankers, researchers have shown that fewer than 10 percent of executives can avoid the winner's curse. For a convenient summary of the research, see Max H. Bazerman and Margaret A. Neale, *Negotiating Rationally* (New York: Free Press, 1992), pp. 49–55.

What you really need is a way of losing without appearing to give in too quickly. Use this simple approach the next time:

How to Lose Graciously

1. *Take time to make sure you understand the other party correctly.* Accepting the first offer right away sends the wrong signal. In a face-to-face situation, listen carefully, ask questions, get as many details as you can. Remember, you aren't using questions to disguise objections; you are honestly seeking information.

When you are not in a face-to-face situation, take your time to think of some questions. When you acknowledge the proposal, attach a list of questions you would like answered. Don't use the questions to disguise objections; you are still gathering information.

2. *Take time to study the proposal.* This is easy when you are negotiating by mail; simply don't answer for a while.

Things are a little more difficult in face-to-face situations, but you can take a break; excuse yourself, walk away from the table, stretch your legs, and take as much time as you reasonably can.

Managing time calls for careful judgment. You want to take enough time to make the other person think you are studying the offer, but you don't want to take so much time that you annoy the other side unnecessarily. Rely on your knowledge of the situation and the other person, and make a reasoned judgment.

3. *Make a more reasonable counteroffer.* Remember that you've already counted this negotiation as a loss, so don't ask for much. You might get something, and you want to make the other party work a bit.

4. *Listen to the other side's response.* In face-to-face situations, take notes, and ask questions. In other situations, study her response carefully.

5. *Take a little time to study the other side's response.* Use your best judgment—a reasonable amount of time but not so much that you annoy the other party.

6. *Concede graciously with an appropriate rationale.* Explain that you have studied the offer and appreciate the other side's good faith; then list the positive features of the agreement. Always point out something positive for both sides. Then give the other side what she wants, and be on your way. Avoid the temptation to complain about how unfair things are or threaten the other side; leave well enough alone. Remember that you already knew you were going to lose this one, so you can move on with a clean conscience.

YOUR MOVE

Imagine that you have a younger brother who dropped out of college after a year or two. He has drifted from job to job, drinking a lot and running up substantial gambling debts. He recently got a job and it looks as if he may clean up his act. However, he needs a car for work, and his has broken down. He wants to borrow $800 from you for repairs. What do you do?

You work for a nonunion company. Your boss has been fair and reasonable but is under a lot of financial pressure. Nine weeks ago, he fired the junior clerk and has asked you to run errands on your way to and from work. You agreed, but now he wants you to run errands on your lunch hour. What do you do?

The property line between your home and an obnoxious neighbor is marked by a shared retaining wall. The wall has begun to crumble since he built a swimming pool near its base, and repairs have been a bone of contention. You were delighted to learn that he has taken a new job in another state and sold his home. The fact that he will be gone is a real plus, in your book. However, he has demanded that you help pay for repairs to the retaining wall. It turns out that the new buyers have a contingency in their offer: They will buy the home only if the wall is repaired within thirty days. Your neighbor estimates costs at $2,500 and expects you to pay $2,000 since you are "on the uphill side." Now what?

 ## ANALYSIS

The case of the feckless brother is one of the toughest you may ever face. Here's how we read the situation. If you don't have the money, there is no issue; you can't help anyway. If you do have the money, there may be other relationships to consider. Perhaps your spouse or parents are keeping an eye on your spending as well. If those complications aren't present, we would say the issue is important to you so you need to find a winning response. The relationship is important to you as well; he's your brother, after all. So you need to find a solution where he wins. This calls for a win-win solution, unless there is some kind of time pressure. Under time pressure, fall back to win-lose or lose-win.

The demanding boss is another tough problem. The issue is important to you; your time is getting eaten up, and there are probably a number of consequences. The relationship is important as well; your job may be on the line. Fortunately, time doesn't seem to be a major issue. You've let this go on for several weeks already, so there is no need to rush now. We recommend a problem-solving discussion with your boss looking for a win-win solution. You can always fall back to a win-lose approach (like taking legal action) later. For the time being, give your boss a chance to change his ways.

We hope you told your neighbor to take a hike (a win-lose strategy). You value the issue—your money—but couldn't care less about the relationship. Time is in your favor here; he, not you, is facing a deadline. He isn't likely to cancel the sale since he has a job elsewhere. He might take you to small-claims court, but that takes time, and he would have to return to town for the hearing. And even if you lose in court, you are likely to get a fairer distribution of expenses than he proposed. He might be a danger to you or your family, but the chances are remote, and you can take other steps to protect yourself. All told, it looks like you should refuse to pay anything.

2

The Blue-Chip Negotiator

In every game, there are some qualities players must have. Without them, it's almost impossible to be a good player. For football players, size, strength, and speed are essential. Grace and agility are keys to other sports. And board games require knowledge, concentration, and strategy.

Each game has its own requirements, and you need to have them if you expect to be a winner. You may be able to get along without a few of them. (Even small, weak, slow kids can play football, for example.) But getting along is about all you can expect. Without the necessary characteristics, you can play in sandlots but will never make it to the big leagues. There are other consequences as well: You will lose more often than you like, and you may never have as much fun as you should.

All this is true of negotiation, too. Some fundamental characteristics are essential to success. Without them, you will never be a blue-chip negotiator. You will negotiate time and again (you can't avoid it in our society), but you will never make it to the big leagues. Worse, you will lose more often than you like, and you may never have much fun at it.

Now here's the good news: Developing the characteristics you need to be a top-flight negotiator is a lot more practical than developing the characteristics you need to excel in other games. Everyone can get a better deal through negotiation; that's a given in our society. And, we think, everybody has the potential to be a top-flight negotiator. The essential characteristics are easy to identify, and you can develop them relatively quickly. In fact, you've probably got many of them already. You started polishing the others the instant you began reading this book. Practice helps, and our society gives you lots of opportunities. Experiment on small matters before you tackle bigger issues.

What does it take to be an outstanding negotiator? Our research and experience point to six fundamentals:

1. A positive attitude
2. Knowledge of the negotiation process
3. An understanding of people
4. A grasp of your subject
5. Some creativity
6. A set of communication skills

Each item is critical. This chapter helps you understand each. Before you read further, take a few minutes to complete the following quiz. Your answers will help create a personal profile—a snapshot of sorts—of your current attributes. No one else will see your scores unless you want them to. Be honest with yourself. Further on in the chapter, we explain how scoring works.

Personal Negotiation Profile

Answer each of the items on a sheet of paper by recording the number from the following scale that most accurately reflects your experiences.

5 = never   4 = seldom   3 = some of the time
2 = often   1 = always

1. I feel angry or anxious going into negotiation.   1 2 3 4 5
2. When negotiating, I like to skip the small talk
   and get right down to business.   1 2 3 4 5
3. I am surprised by the views other people
   express in negotiations.   1 2 3 4 5
4. The people with whom I deal are better
   informed than I am.   1 2 3 4 5
5. I feel trapped by the deals I negotiate; I don't
   like the results, but I don't have any other
   choices.   1 2 3 4 5
6. In negotiating, I do more than half of the
   talking.   1 2 3 4 5
7. The people with whom I negotiate are hostile
   and/or defensive.   1 2 3 4 5

8. When negotiating, I get caught off guard; I don't know what's coming next and feel like things are out of control.   1   2   3   4   5
9. I am uncomfortable dealing with people who are different from me.   1   2   3   4   5
10. After negotiation is over, I learn things that I wish I had known before it began.   1   2   3   4   5
11. I think of better arguments to support my position when it's too late to use them.   1   2   3   4   5
12. Other negotiators don't seem to want to listen to me or appreciate my point of view.   1   2   3   4   5
13. I dislike negotiation because no one seems to win.   1   2   3   4   5
14. I am glad when negotiation is done because I know I won't have to deal with the other party again.   1   2   3   4   5
15. I lose my cool when dealing with certain people.   1   2   3   4   5
16. I don't take much time to study the deals I negotiate because finding relevant information takes more time than it's worth.   1   2   3   4   5
17. I feel powerless; I don't like what is happening, but I have to go along.   1   2   3   4   5
18. After negotiating, it is hard for me to recall what the other party wanted and why they wanted it.   1   2   3   4   5

Keep your answer sheet close by as you read the rest of this chapter and learn to:

1. Describe the characteristics needed to be a blue-chip negotiator.
2. Recognize these characteristics in yourself and in others.
3. Identify your own strengths and weaknesses.
4. Create a plan to develop your personal abilities.
5. Cope with other negotiators' strengths and weaknesses.

The Six Essentials

We'll show you how to interpret your scores after looking at each of the essentials more closely.

Essential 1: A Positive Attitude

A positive attitude is the starting point for almost everything you do. If you aren't in the right frame of mind, you can't be an effective negotiator.

Your attitude determines how you conduct yourself in a negotiation. Like most other people, you have a vast number of skills and abilities; you use some a lot of the time and others less frequently, and you may not always be conscious of your choices. Sometimes one set of behaviors feels natural, sometimes another seems right, and sometimes nothing seems to fit. The difference in these situations is your own attitude.

When you are confident and prepared, everything seems easy and natural. When you are unsure of yourself, nothing feels quite right. And when you are angry, hostile, or conflicted, the choices you make are likely to be at war with one another, attitude conflicting with attitude to block effective expression of your desires and prevent effective application of your skills.

Even more important, your attitude often determines how other people respond to you. Inspirational speakers have done a lot to popularize this notion. In their version, you choose what happens to you. If you plan for and anticipate good things, they inevitably come to pass. If you concentrate on possible mishaps, you are likely to have a negative outcome.

In negotiation, something very much like this happens; it's explained by a basic psychological principle, the self-fulfilling prophecy. Studied by researchers for over four decades, the self-fulfilling prophecy exists because we cannot avoid communicating our hopes and fears to the people around us. Most of our communication is nonverbal, conveyed through posture, facial expressions, tone of voice, speaking rate, and vocal inflections. Few people can hide their feelings; moreover, efforts to hide or disguise them send even more noteworthy signals to anyone who pays attention.

Our nonverbal signals are almost always unintentional, but they are seldom ignored by the people with whom we deal. If we feel threatened, our behavior will signal fear or uncertainty, and the other party may rush in to take advantage. Similarly, if we are angry, our behavior will signal hostility, and other players will move to defend themselves. And so it goes, through the whole range of emotions and attitudes. If you approach negotiation with a positive attitude, your behavior will signal confidence, self-assurance, and trustworthiness. Other people will warm to you and support your efforts to make the negotiation a positive, productive experience.

Essential 2: Knowledge of the Negotiation Process

Negotiation is a process, defined by *The Merriam-Webster Dictionary* as "a natural phenomenon marked by gradual changes that lead toward a particular result, or, a series of actions or operations directed toward a particular result." The gradual changes or series of actions that make up the negotiation process form what we call the REPA cycle (Relate, Explore, Propose, Agree). We'll talk about each of these steps in greater detail in Chapter 3, but a brief overview of the process here will help you see particular skills and applications in their proper context.

Skipping steps works to your disadvantage, even when you are "anxious to get down to business." We've heard many clients, students, and salespeople use this phrase because they think "real" negotiation starts at the third step. In other words, they don't think they are negotiating until there is a proposal on the table. For this shortsightedness, they often pay a heavy price. Without having established trust needed to communicate freely and without exploring common interests, they haven't gotten enough information to reach a mutually satisfying agreement.

Moreover, everyone makes assumptions about the negotiation process. Your assumptions can trap you if they don't accurately reflect the situation. For example, skilled players often use small talk to gain critical information. If you don't realize that negotiation begins with the relationship, you are vulnerable to crafty negotiators who do. As you chat before the negotiation begins, you may well inadvertently divulge vital information without getting anything in return.

Essential 3: An Understanding of People

A good understanding of other people is vital. Negotiation is about reaching agreement, and you are not done until the other person agrees. Knowing how other players work—what makes them tick—is invaluable because it helps to conduct negotiation in an agreeable manner, present your proposals in an attractive way, avoid offending other players, and protect yourself from traps they may set.

Here is a brief list of the things you should know about the other party in any negotiation:

- What motivates them? What are their needs and values?
- How do they approach social interaction? Do they prefer directness and frankness, or do the rely on misdirection and implication?
- How do they use body language? Are they naturally free and open, or is their behavior rigid and controlled?
- What is their attitude toward time? Do they rush to reach agreement or take time to explore options?
- How do they feel about the use of power? Is it acceptable practice or something to be shunned or avoided?
- What characterizes their decision-making process? Is it rational and objective, or intuitive and subjective?

We'll tell you how to answer these questions and many more in Chapters 3 and 6. For now, you need to realize that understanding people is vital. You may be good at working with people from your own culture because you share a common background. However, we all need to be particularly sensitive when we deal with people from other cultures, especially since we have so many opportunities to deal with them.

Essential 4: Grasp of the Subject

A grasp of the subject is the fourth characteristic of an accomplished negotiator. Top-flight negotiators usually have very specific knowledge about the value of the things with which they deal, the consequences of different agreements they might negotiate, and alternative ways of getting what they want. They understand that knowledge is power and base their judgments on experience, education, and research. We'll show you what you need to know and how to learn it in Chapter 3. Chapter 7 adds the concept of competitive intelligence—information about the other player's view of the situation—which is particularly important in some transactions. For now, you need to realize that you are at a disadvantage whenever the other player knows more about the subject than you do.

Essential 5: Creativity

Creativity, a vital antidote to a common error, is probably overlooked more often than any other characteristic. Many people think you should settle on a solution before you negotiate and use bargaining

🗽 OBJECT LESSON

A major insurance company learned the value of detailed knowledge in a transaction that cost it dearly. The company holds the mortgage on a downtown hotel in a very desirable area. Although business is good, the hotel operator seldom made payments on time. Unable to get him to commit to a regular payment schedule, the insurance company threatened to foreclose on the hotel. They hoped to teach the operator a lesson while adding to their profits by operating the hotel themselves.

The operator asked only one question: "Where will you park the guests' cars?" He knew, and the insurance company didn't, that the parking structure was part of a separate partnership fully under his control. If the insurance company foreclosed on the hotel, he would close the structure, effectively putting the hotel out of business.

Faced with this situation, the insurance company stopped foreclosure proceedings, forgave back payments, and renegotiated the mortgage on terms dictated by the operator.

The Lesson: You are at risk whenever you know less about a
              subject than the other player does.

to make the other player accept your proposal. In other words, decide what you want and then use your skills to force it on the other party.

Skilled negotiators, in contrast, seldom lock themselves in. They may develop some positions before negotiation, but they are always tentative so negotiation doesn't involve arguing over one-sided, predetermined positions. Instead, negotiation becomes a genuine problem-solving process working to satisfy the interests of both players. Here is what creativity contributes to negotiation:

- Novel, innovative solutions that characterize win-win agreements
- Persuasive reasons to support your own position
- Solutions to implementation problems that turn up once general solutions are agreed upon
- Alternatives to negotiated agreement that increase your power by making you less dependent on the deal

These are all vital elements of negotiation. Developing your own creative ability is the best way to generate them.

GOOD TO KNOW

Creativity is important whenever you are confronted with a difficult problem. One of our colleagues and his coauthor have proposed seven principles to guide your search for innovative solutions:

1. Each problem is unique and requires a unique solution.
2. Focusing on purposes helps strip away nonessential aspects of a problem.
3. Having a target solution in the future gives direction to near-term solutions and infuses them with larger purposes.
4. Every problem is part of a larger system of problems, and solving one problem inevitably leads to another.
5. Excessive data gathering . . . will probably prevent the discovery of some excellent alternatives.
6. Those who will carry out and use the solution should be intimately and continuously involved in its development.
7. The only way to preserve the vitality of a solution is to build in and then monitor a program of continual change.

From Gerald Nadler and Shozo Hibino, *Breakthrough Thinking* (Rocklin, Calif.: Prima Publishing and Communications, 1990).

Essential 6: Communication

Communication is the final essential. You can't negotiate without communicating. Right? Everyone knows that the best negotiators are skilled communicators, and the more skilled you are, the more you can accomplish. Here is the one piece of information we need to add to what you already know: Communication involves much more than expressing your own views. In fact, listening and observation are at least as important as speaking.

Taking time to find out what the other person wants shows good faith; it shows that you really want to negotiate, not just push your own position. At the same time, listening helps build the foundation for a relationship. It shows that you value the other person and take him seriously. In addition, listening makes it possible to find win-win solutions. Finding win-win solutions requires knowing what the other party wants before you make a proposal; you will never learn what you need to know if you don't listen carefully. Finally, listening may give you a strategic advantage. Knowledge is power, especially

---

"If you ask a question on a particular subject and the answer is unsatisfactory, the best response is none at all. If you are seeking more information, or a different kind of information, ask for it by remaining silent.

"Silence is a void, and people feel an overwhelming need to fill it. If someone has finished speaking and you don't play along by taking up your end of the dialogue, after only the slightest pause that person will automatically start to elaborate. Eventually they may say what you want to hear."

Mark H. McCormack, *What They Don't Teach You at Harvard Business School* (New York: Bantam Books, 1984), pp. 109–110.

---

in negotiation, and you learn more when you are listening than when you are talking. Opposing negotiators may even hang themselves by exposing weaknesses in their positions if you let them talk long enough.

 **GOOD TO KNOW**

Recent research has emphasized the importance of nonverbal communication in creating situations in which people can work together comfortably. Critical behaviors include getting close to the other person, touching when and where appropriate, facing the other person directly, relaxing, nodding your head in agreement, smiling, maintaining eye contact, and varying your voice to express feelings.

For a summary of this research, see J. K. Burgoon, D. B. Butler, and W. G. Woodall, *Nonverbal Communication: The Unspoken Dialogue* (New York: Harper & Row, 1989).

Interpreting Your Profile

Now that you are familiar with each of the essential attributes, interpreting your scores from the quiz in this chapter is easy. To compute your score for each attribute, copy your answers on to Exhibit 2-1, and add your scores for each column to see how you do on the six essentials.

Exhibit 2-1. Scoring the six essentials of negotiation.

Positive Attitude	Negotiation Process	Understanding People	Grasp of Subject	Creativity	Communication
Question 1. ___	Question 2. ___	Question 3. ___	Question 4. ___	Question 5. ___	Question 6. ___
Question 7. ___	Question 8. ___	Question 9. ___	Question 10. ___	Question 11. ___	Question 12. ___
Question 13. ___	Question 14. ___	Question 15. ___	Question 16. ___	Question 17. ___	Question 18. ___
Total Score ___	___	___	___	___	___

The lower your score is, the more you can do to improve your negotiation skills. Keep the following guide in mind as you look at your scores in each area. If your score is from 12 to 15, you are doing pretty well on this item; some growth may be possible, but it is not needed, and this area should have a relatively low priority. Scores from 7 to 11 are about average; you are typical of most other people in this regard. You can grow here, but change is not urgent. Scores 6 and below indicate that you can grow quite a bit in this area. You may experience considerable difficulty in negotiation, and growth in this area should have a high priority.

Coping With Your Own Frailties

The profile you have created will help you focus your efforts to grow. Knowing your relative strengths and weaknesses tells you where to concentrate your efforts. Use the following guide to identify the chapters that call for your attention the most:

To develop skills in this area:	Turn to the following materials:
Positive attitude	Introduction and Chapter 1
Knowledge of the negotiation process	Chapters 3 and 5, plus particular applications in Chapters 7, 8, 9, and 10
Understanding of people	Chapter 6
Grasp of your subject	Chapter 4
Creativity	Chapter 4
Communication skills	Chapters 3, 5, and 6

Coping With Strengths and Weaknesses in Others

You will inevitably begin to notice strengths and weaknesses in the people with whom you deal. A few people are strong in all six areas and a few people are weak in all six. Most people will be scattered between the extremes—strong in some areas, weak in others, with lots of average or middling scores.

Learn to enjoy working with the very skilled negotiators. You can learn a great deal from them, and the game gets better when you are evenly matched. Don't feel intimidated; you know how your skills compare to theirs, and you know what homework you need to do when you deal with them.

Recognizing particular shortcomings in other negotiators also suggests some strategies for dealing with them. Hostile, argumentative, rigid, and inflexible negotiators are generally trying to cover their own weaknesses, and the skills we set out in this book will position you to help them by playing coach, counselor, and mediator. You can shape their expectations by carefully explaining what you want to accomplish and how. You can also suggest several alternative procedures and let them select the ones with which they are most comfortable. Chapter 5 alerts you to some of the tricks they may try and suggests ways of protecting yourself. Suggestions for dealing with difficult people in Chapter 6 prepare you to play negotiation jujitsu. You don't have to fight them; simply turn their aggressive behavior to your advantage. When the other person insists on winning, let her win on your terms.

 YOUR MOVE

Interpreting your personal negotiation profile will help you plan your personal development. Here are three representative profiles. What would you suggest each person do to further develop his or her abilities?

John

Positive Attitude	8
Negotiation Process	10
Understanding People	9
Grasp of Subject	11
Creativity	10
Communication	9

Maria

Positive Attitude	12
Negotiation Process	10
Understanding People	7
Grasp of Subject	3
Creativity	9
Communication	11

Jesse

Positive Attitude	12
Negotiation Process	10
Understanding People	9
Grasp of Subject	9
Creativity	14
Communication	8

 ANALYSIS

The three profiles are typical of those we have seen in classes, seminars, and personal consultations. Each of the participants should have a unique agenda for developing his or her skills.

John's profile is well balanced and similar to those of people who are doing relatively well in all areas. We would suggest that John continue working at his own pace, reading about negotiation in general, practicing his communication skills when he has a chance, and preparing for specific negotiations when they come up.

Maria's profile is well balanced in most respects, but we see one real concern—her grasp of the subjects on which she negotiates. We suspect that she often finds herself at a disadvantage when dealing with savvy negotiators because they are better prepared than she is. We would recommend that Maria concentrate on specific deals, using the guides in Chapter 4 to help her prepare for each. She may want to expand her contacts with knowledgable professionals and pay attention to values, terms, and conditions in deals others have negotiated.

Jesse's profile is as strong or stronger than those of his colleagues, and we would look forward to dealing with him. His greatest strength is creativity and his talents might be wasted in routine negotiations. We would be inclined to use him as part of a negotiating team focusing on particularly important deals. We think other team members can learn a lot from him and can help him avoid the trap of being too creative. Jesse's profile also suggests that he could be an outstanding mediator, and we would look to improving his communication skills so that he can be more effective in such a role.

3

The Basic Game Plan

Now that you have a general understanding of negotiation, it's time to put your knowledge to use. We have found it is easiest for people to get started if they have a specific game plan—a general approach that they can follow no matter what else happens. The basic game plan won't take advantage of all of your strengths, but it will allow you to begin playing quickly and with confidence. Later chapters, especially Chapter 5, introduce some advanced elements of play—strategies and tactics that will help you capitalize on your own strengths and avoid the traps skillful opponents may set for you. Here is what you will find in this chapter:

1. An ideal game plan—the steps to follow in any negotiation
2. The tools and techniques to use at each step in the game
3. Some suggestions for conducting negotiating sessions
4. A set of special tactics to help keep the process moving when a negotiation appears to be deadlocked
5. Some means of dealing with people who refuse to go along

The Ideal Game Plan

Skilled negotiators and careful observers have learned that there is a natural order to negotiation. Follow this order, and you can be reasonably sure that the negotiation will progress logically, leading to a reasonably fair and equitable solution—other things being equal. Depart from this order, and you have reason to be on guard. In fact, skilled negotiators depart from this order only when the switch gives them an advantage. That alone is a powerful argument for sticking with this order, especially when you are starting out.

Here are the key steps in the order:

Relate

↓

Explore

↓

Propose

↓

Agree

Keep in mind that this order is neutral; it doesn't favor either side. When you use it, there is no reason to hide or disguise your plan. You may want to share it with the other side and encourage them to follow the same order. In fact, discussing the order with them provides a convenient way of organizing the entire negotiation. Additionally, the order is a logical reflection of the tasks to be accomplished at each step in the process:

1. *Building a relationship.* Building a relationship is an essential first step because it provides a context in which the other player will feel comfortable sharing information. We're not talking about a friendship, although that is an added advantage. Setting an appropriate tone or climate and introducing the procedures you plan to use will make the negotiation run much more smoothly than otherwise.

2. *Exploring the interests of both sides.* Exploration often takes more time than you might expect because both players commonly begin by

---

"The basic problem in negotiation lies not in conflicting positions, but in the conflict between each side's needs, desires, concerns, and fears. . . . Such desires and concerns are *interests*. Interests motivate people; they are the silent movers behind the hubbub of position. Your position is something you have decided upon. Your interests are what caused you to so decide."

Roger Fisher and William Ury with Bruce Patton, *Getting to Yes*, 2d ed. (New York: Penguin Books, 1992), pp. 40–41.

stating their positions. Listen carefully, and you will see that the positions are actually predetermined, one-sided approaches to solving the problem that bring you to the table. Getting past the positions and talking about the reasons for them is essential to crafting a mutually satisfactory solution. In fact, the distinction between positions and interests is a key to all successful negotiation, and you shouldn't move on to the next step until you know what the other party wants and why.

3. *Developing proposals.* Proposals that emerge at this stage differ considerably from those with which you started. Your objective here is to see that there is at least once concrete proposal that addresses all of your underlying interests. Make sure the proposal is fully spelled out and that you understand all of its provisions before you move ahead. Writing the proposal in clear, nontechnical language is often the easiest way to make sure it is understood. You can always work from an existing agreement or contract, editing earlier provisions and adding new ones to satisfy both players.

4. *Reaching agreement.* This final step often involves plain old horse trading, compromising, creating alternatives, and swapping one provision for another. The easiest approach is to work through the proposed agreement one provision at a time. If you have a written proposal, it's useful to have both parties initial the provisions as agreement is reached and then sign off on the whole document when all of the constituents have been initialed.

Most people are comfortable with the REPA cycle. It will become second nature to you once you have practiced it a few times. In fact, you will probably be amazed at how quickly everything falls into place and how natural the process feels. From time to time, you'll run into others who will want to follow a different order. Inexperienced negotiators often say that they want to "skip the small talk and get down to business." More than anything else, this approach marks them as novices, and they may be easy prey for more experienced negotiators. Their mistake is thinking that the "real work" begins only when a proposal is on the table. In fact, American negotiators are often criticized by foreigners for not taking time to establish relationships before trying to work out a deal.

In our experience, most of the inexperienced negotiators will go along with you if you simply explain why the first couple of steps are important. You might simply explain the order like this:

"I understand your desire to get down to business. However, I'll feel more comfortable once we get to know each other. And, I think we can find a way to make everyone happy if we have a better idea of what we are both looking for."

REPA Tools and Techniques

Now that you understand the ideal game plan and what you want to accomplish at each step, let's equip you with the tools and techniques that researchers have identified to help you get the information you need and promote agreement at each step in the process.

Tools and Techniques to Help You Relate

Remember that the aim of the first step in the negotiation process is to establish a relationship—a context that will make it possible for both parties to share the information needed to make negotiations go smoothly. This step is often overlooked, but it is critical because it sets the tone or climate for the entire negotiation. A good start will make everything else run smoothly. With a firm foundation, the negotiators will be able to solve problems that might otherwise prevent agreement.

You probably already use many relationship-building techniques in your daily conversations. In our experience, four are particularly important:

1. *Paying attention.* Your attention signals interest in the other person and opens the door for a genuine, sincere conversation. Watch skilled listeners, and you will see that they are paying close attention to the other person. What shows that they are paying attention? Here are the keys: an erect posture, leaning slightly toward the other player, consistent eye contact, and appropriate body motion, including gestures that reinforce and demonstrate understanding.

2. *Conversation openers.* These are nothing more than the topics of polite conversation used in talking to a stranger. They are neutral, unthreatening topics that most people find easy to discuss: small talk about sports and hobbies, the context or situation, sincere compliments, and references to current events, for example. With a little thought, you can easily generate a list of topics you and the other party feel comfortable discussing.

3. *Renewal strategies.* These are the kinds of things old friends discuss when they have a chance to catch up with one another: experiences they have shared in the past, common interests, and the health and well-being of family members and friends, for example.

4. *Reciprocal disclosure.* This is an academic term, but we use it because nothing else conveys our meaning as accurately. While you are attempting to establish a relationship with someone, that person will probably be trying to establish a relationship with you. If you expect the other person to talk about family, friends, and interests, you need to do the same. In other words, when someone shares personal information, you need to *reciprocate*, to share information about yourself. Make sure your disclosures are consistent with the nature of the situation and your relationship with the other person, but feel free to talk about anything that is important to you.

Tools and Techniques to Help You Explore

Once both parties are comfortable with the relationship, it's time to begin exploring the other party's needs and interests. Don't rush to put a proposal on the table. Rather, begin by making sure you understand the situation from the other person's point of view:

- What items are important to him?
- Why is he participating in the negotiation?
- What does he hope to accomplish?
- Who will be looking over his shoulder and evaluating the outcome of the negotiation?
- Does he face deadlines?
- What are the consequences of failing to reach agreement?

Looking at that list of questions, you can see why it is so critical to establish a relationship first. If the other party doesn't trust you, he will be reluctant to share information that might be used against him. And even if you have established a good working relationship, he may want to limit how much he tells you.

It's natural for people to be guarded in a negotiation. However, there are three powerful techniques you can use to explore the situation:

1. *Open questions*, that is, those that require more than a simple yes or no. Closed questions can be answered with a single word or

phrase—for example, "Do you approve of the grievance procedure?" or "Do you plan to buy a new computer this year?" There is nothing wrong with closed questions. In fact, they have a powerful role in negotiation; they are used to make sure you understand particular parts of a proposal and to confirm agreement. Open questions, however, force those on the other side to give you an answer that may reveal something important about their needs, concerns, and interests. Look at the following questions:

"Why do you think we should reopen negotiations at this time?"
"Who is affected by the proposed changes?"
"How will you implement the new policy?"
"When would you like to close the deal?"
"What do you think is important here?"

All of thes questions require an extended answer. That is a characteristic of all open questions. In general, any question that begins with one of the key words—*why, who, how, when,* and *what*—is an open question. They are the stock and trade of the skilled negotiator while exploring the other party's needs, interests, and concerns.

2. *Probes* are ways of getting the other side to extend or add to answers. They are used less often than questions, but they are even more powerful because they often go unnoticed by the other person, who will often tell you far more than she realizes. Here are some of the most useful types:

- Silent attention, or keeping your mouth shut. When the other player finishes a sentence, pay attention but remain silent. The pause signals the other person to keep talking, and most will oblige. We have seen skilled negotiators keep another person talking for twenty minutes or more using nothing more than silent attention.
- Neutral phrases—"um hmm," "yes," "oh," and "I see." They show the other person that you are interested in what he is saying and gives him the opportunity to keep going.
- Mirror statements, to show that you are interested and invite the other person to continue. For example, if the other person says, "We need a significant increase in compensation this year," you might echo, "Significant increase," and wait to see what happens next. There is a good chance that the other person will explain what she means by "significant increase,"

and you may even find out why that is important to her at this time.

- Internal summaries, used after an extended discussion to make sure that you understand the other party and give him a chance to add anything that he may have overlooked. For example, you might summarize a conversation like this:

"Let me make sure I understand you correctly. You need a significant increase in compensation, something on the order of 7 percent, because several members of your union are agitating for a change and the national office has recommended that target."

Pause when you are done, and the other party will correct any misunderstandings and may add other important pieces of information.

3. *Observations* are a potent source of information. By watching the other person's reactions, you can quickly tell which topics are most important to her, what issues are likely to be particularly sensitive, and whether she feels time pressure.

Tools and Techniques to Help You Propose

During the third stage of the negotiation, aim to get a concrete proposal on the table, one that addresses all of the core issues and leaves nothing to chance. For many negotiators, this is the heart of the process. You can already see why this phase will go much more smoothly once you have taken time to build a relationship and explore the underlying interests and concerns.

Negotiators with whom we have worked use two very different strategies at this stage. Some say never make the first offer. They wait for the other player to move so they have a base to work from. Others prefer to be the first to put a proposal on the table. They think their proposal anchors the discussion, establishing a range for the final solution.

We have seen both strategies work well and think the choice is largely a matter of personal preference. Here are six points to remember, whichever strategy you prefer:

1. *Always do your homework before the negotiation.* You should know how similar matters have been decided in the past, what kinds

⭐ OBJECT LESSON

Du Pont made a classic first-offer error in 1985. Anxious to reduce its workforce by about 5 percent, Du Pont offered a generous early retirement program, adding five years to both the age and service records of employees who left early. The offer was so attractive that nearly 10 percent left; at some Conoco refineries, over 16 percent took the offer. This blunder cost over $125 million, not counting bonuses paid to keep some valued employees from retiring and the cost of hiring new people to fill some critical vacancies.

The lesson: Be careful; you just might get what you ask for!

From Bruce Nash and Allan Zullo, *The Misfortune 500* (New York: Pocket Books, 1988), p. 2.

of terms and conditions are typical, what your best alternative to negotiated agreement is, and your own bottom line.

2. When making an offer, *start at the limit but imply flexibility.* For example, if buying a business, make an offer at the lower reasonable limit but signal willingness to negotiate. If you go too low, you may offend the other player; if you don't imply flexibility, the other party may conclude you aren't worth dealing with.

3. Whether you are making or receiving an offer, *always be prepared to state reasons for your proposal.* Although the other person may not be convinced by your reasons, they give her something to work with and may provide ammunition if she has to justify accepting the offer of someone else.

4. *Never accept the first offer of the other side.* He has probably begun at his limit and probably will move if you don't accept immediately. Accepting the first offer may leave the other party dissatisfied because he thinks he could have done better.

5. *Always use a checklist with all of the key issues.* Make sure the proposal is complete and addresses all of the critical issues.

6. Use closed questions to *make sure you understand the offer correctly.* "Will you make the first payment on July 1?" "Are the appliances included?" and "The first shipment will arrive next Monday, right?" are all closed questions. In fact, almost any question that begins with a verb is a closed question and will force the other party to give a precise answer.

Make sure that you understand all elements of the proposal before you move on to the next step. Never say yes or no to any part of a proposal you don't understand fully. Be careful here: Some negotiators will try to trap you into accepting part of a proposal by suggesting you reach agreement on "minor points" before working out "other details." Our advice is simple: Don't do it!

Even if some elements cannot be tied down, as often happens in complex business deals, make sure that the proposal includes an explicit procedure for making decisions later.

If the proposal is incomplete or unclear, loop back to the propose stage by saying something like,

> "I realize that you would like to reach agreement, but I'm still not sure about something. What do you mean by _____?"

You can loop back as many times as you need to.

Tools and Techniques to Help You Agree

Reaching agreement is the final stage of the negotiation process. The process is often easier than you can imagine because you have done so much preliminary work building a relationship, exploring interests, and developing a comprehensive proposal. Sometimes reaching agreement comes down to horse trading—give a little, get a little. At other times, reaching agreement requires creative problem solving. The choice depends on your strategy (we'll talk about it more fully in Chapter 5). However, at this point, you need to be able to disagree without being disagreeable, give good reasons for your position, and make concessions gracefully.

Disagreeing without being disagreeable is a real art. A blunt, unreasoning NO! can undo all of your groundwork. A careless refusal can turn the negotiation into a debate that no one wins. Worse, an outright refusal can become a source of contention so that the other party will stick to her guns, no matter what.

To avoid getting stuck in a futile debate or a test of wills, try this formula whenever you need to reject a portion of a proposal:

> "I know just how you *feel*."
> "In fact, I *felt* that way myself."
> "But let me tell you what I *found*."

You may recognize this as the "feel, felt, found" formula that skilled salespeople use because it helps the other person to hear no without feeling the need to fight. Follow the statement with good reasons for your position, and the negotiation can proceed smoothly in spite of your rejection.

Presenting good reasons for your position gives the other person something to work with in refining his proposal. The reasons also make it possible for the other player to justify an unfavorable outcome when he has to report to someone else.

A good reason is anything that supports your point of view and appears reasonable to the other player, even if he doesn't agree. Don't feel the need to overwhelm him with reasons. In fact, some research suggests that skilled negotiators often use just one or two reasons, whereas less skilled negotiators use a laundry list. Here are three examples:

> "I realize you would like us to accept a 5 percent wage cut, but I can't because it would violate our agreement with the national office and our members have already voted to accept nothing more than 2 percent."

> "I see that the service guarantee is important to you. Unfortunately, I can't accept those terms because we have already cut our price to the bone."

> "Of course, it would be great if I accepted the Johnson project. But my key engineer is scheduled to retire next month, and the personnel office has said that I can't replace her."

All three of these reasons are clear and concise and give the other party room to maneuver. In the first example, the company might propose to reduce other benefits, demanding only a 2 percent wage cut. The customer in the second example might agree that price concessions have been adequate compensation or propose an alternative. And the manager in the final example might get Personnel to change its ruling if his supervisor will accept the new project. These are all possible outcomes. The important point is that presenting good reasons always leaves the other party some maneuvering room and a way to justify negative results to other interested players.

Finally, there may come a point where you need to make concessions gracefully. Even though particular points may be difficult for you, you may have to accept them because the overall agreement is worthwhile. Or, you may be over a barrel and need to accept the agreement. Whatever the case, make concessions in a way that does not compromise your relationship with the other side or endanger future negotiations. Accept the best you can get, and accept it gracefully, without whining, whimpering, blaming, or threatening. Some examples will show you what we mean:

> "We've worked hard to make this negotiation productive. I'm still not happy with the 5 percent cut, but it is the best we can do right now."

> "I appreciate your efforts to work around the service guarantee issue. I understand why it's important to you, and I will do what I can to sell it to my boss."

> "Completing the Johnson project without another engineer will be difficult. But I see your point: No one else can do it as well as we can, and I'll give it my best."

Conducting the Negotiation Session

Many of your negotiations will involve players who share your culture. The more they have in common with you, the less you need to worry about your behavior because they share your assumptions about negotiation and interaction. As a result, much of what you do during a negotiation session is just plain common sense, based on your training and experience. For example, the way you dress, the way you introduce yourself to other players, greetings and handshakes, smoking and drinking, and meeting times are all governed by social conventions. Conduct yourself as you normally would, and you should have few difficulties. Nevertheless, there are a few special situations to be aware of. The advice that follows is adequate for the overwhelming majority of negotiations, but you may encounter special cases that call for advanced skills. To prepare for negotiations with players from other countries or who gain advantage by breaking the rules, look ahead to Chapter 6.

Team Negotiations

Many negotiations are one-on-one affairs, but some will be team events, with several players representing each side. The more people who are involved, the more important it is to observe basic meeting etiquette. We think you know the drill, but here are some pointers to keep in mind:

- Make sure everyone on your team knows when and where the meeting will be held, how they should prepare and what they should bring, and what their role is in your game plan.
- Arrive on time, prepared to participate.
- Know the agenda, and stick to it unless something extraordinary happens.
- Begin with introductions, welcomes, and pleasantries, but remember that everything you and your teammates say, even casual remarks made before there is a proposal on the table, is part of the negotiation.

Their Turf or Yours?

There are advantages to conducting negotiations on neutral ground, where neither side has the home field advantage. A conference center, hotel, restaurant, mediator's office, or other neutral site is generally easy to arrange and promotes an environment of comfort and equality. However, being on your home ground also has advantages to *you:* access to resources and materials, status symbols demonstrating your importance, and the opportunity to arrange the meeting space to your advantage. At the same time, be wary when you are meeting on the other side's home turf. Know that at least some of the cards will be stacked against you, and come prepared with an excuse to postpone the negotiation if the situation seems too lopsided.

Interruptions and Other Distractions

Managing interruptions and distractions is a matter of both courtesy and strategy. Courtesy dictates minimizing both. If you are on your home field, close your door, instruct your secretary to hold your calls, clear your desk, and concentrate on the task at hand. On neutral turf, arrange for the staff to guarantee privacy and freedom from distractions. When your are on the other side's ground, the extent to which they clear the deck tells you a lot: the importance they attach to you and the negotiation, what they will be like to deal with after agreement is reached, and the tactics they are planning to employ.

Managing interruptions and distractions has a strategic component as well when you use them to your advantage. For example, if the other side attempts to pressure you or acts as if you are in a weaker position, well-timed interruptions signal your willingness to postpone the negotiation and restore equality.

Calling time out, taking a break, and postponing the negotiation involve both courtesy and strategy. Marathon negotiations favor players with the most stamina, and courtesy suggests frequent breaks so both sides feel refreshed. Similarly, creativity is hard work, and it's a good idea to take a break when both sides have run out of ideas. There are other reasons, as well to take a break:

- Things have become confusing and you need time to sort them out.
- You don't know an answer and need to do some research.
- The other side is so rigid that further work at this time is futile.
- Emotions have flared, and comments are beginning to get personal.
- The other side is pressuring you for a decision, and you need to find out if they're hiding anything (and what it is).
- The other side is behaving in an inconsistent manner; you suspect there is a hidden agenda or an unidentified third party involved.
- The other side requests a break, and you don't have a good reason to object.

 GOOD TO KNOW

Many people are annoyed when someone interrupts them. Yet research suggests that interruptions, irritating as they are, make valuable contributions to the conversation. Analyzing 255 interruptions taken from conversations, Carol W. Kennedy and Carl T. Camden found that 38 percent showed agreement, 24 percent changed the subject, 19 percent signaled disagreement, 11 percent provided clarification, and only 8 percent were used to make light of the subject.

From "A New Look at Interruptions," *Western Journal of Speech Communication* 47 (1983): 45–58.

Telephone Negotiation

We prefer face-to-face negotiation, but sometimes the telephone has to be used. When you find yourself negotiating over the telephone, be sure you know who is on the line, whether the call is being recorded, who is calling the plays for the other side, and who may overhear the conversation. We get particularly nervous when the other side uses a speaker telephone. When we don't know what's going on on the other end, we often postpone the negotiation or avoid making commitments.

Negotiating in Social Situations

Negotiating in social situations calls for special sensitivity. Parties, golf games, lunches and dinners, and other outings are wonderful opportunities to meet and get to know the other side. If the other side isn't prepared to go beyond social pleasantries, your pushing for a decision can compromise the relationship. We prefer to use such social contacts to establish a relationship and begin exploring common interests, but we stop short of proposing and trying to reach agreement. When you are unsure of the other side's intentions, ask. You should push for more only in the most extraordinary circumstances.

Social Blunders

Be prepared to help other players recover from embarrassment when necessary. Everyone makes a mistake from time to time, and social blunders include spilled coffee, overly enthusiastic handshakes that crush the other player's hand, inappropriate words and phrases, offensive jokes, inadvertent racial or sexual references, and bodily noises. Naturally, you will avoid these blunders yourself, but you can also help the other player recover with at least some dignity. Why? His embarrassment can derail the negotiation, and he may be uncomfortable dealing with you in the future. Our advice is to ignore the blunder if you can, change the subject when possible, and tell an unrelated joke to divert attention when all else fails. By the way, remember that some crafty negotiators will deliberately make blunders to throw you off your guard. If you find yourself helping the other player recover, you may be dealing with one of the sharks. When that happens, flip to Chapter 6, where we tell you how to get them to straighten up.

Breaking Deadlocks

Even the most experienced negotiators sometimes run into problems that seem unsoluble. The interests of the parties are such that they simply can't reach agreement. Even when both players really want to find a solution, and even when both have worked in an orderly, systematic way, they still may reach a point where neither will move. Both are so firmly entrenched in their positions that a deadlock seems inevitable. Things are much worse when one or both try to achieve personal advantage at the expense of the other.

At times like this, you may be tempted to throw up your hands and say, "Well, we gave it our best." When you reach this point, there is no guarantee of success. Even after you have used all the tricks in the book, you may need to give up. However, when the negotiation is important to you, you my want to try some special tactics before giving up and walking away.

Deadlock Breaker 1: Focus on the Problem

Many negotiations reach deadlock because the parties are arguing for different solutions to the same problem. Once they are locked into a debate about which is the better solution, it's hard for them to find other alternatives. They may never find the third solution that would make both parties happy.

Instead of arguing over the solutions, step back and say something like this:

> "We both agree that this is a real problem. Where we differ is in the solutions we favor. Before we give up, let's take a minute or two to review what we know about the problem and see if there isn't some other solution that will satisfy both of us."

Deadlock Breaker 2: Turn Problem Situations Into Choice Situations

Sometimes there doesn't appear to be any acceptable solution to a problem. If the problem is central to the negotiation, the whole process may break down.

When the inability to solve a problem causes a deadlock, try turning the stumbling block into a choice situation. List as many possible solutions as you can think of and then choose the best solution, or even parts of several different solutions. You might say something like this:

> "We really seem to be stuck here; there just doesn't seem to be any way around this problem. Rather than giving up,

> let's brainstorm as many possible solutions as we can
> before we try to pick one."

Then start listing possible solutions without getting into a debate
about the merits of any of them.

Deadlock Breaker 3: Turn Choice Situations Into Problem Situations

Negotiations can break down if the sides can't choose among the
different solutions to a problem. This usually happens when the
parties have proposed several solutions, each of which has both good
and bad features.

You can often get out of this spot by turning attention back to
the problem you were trying to solve. Instead of continuing to argue
about the good and bad features of each solution, turn things around
by asking what you are trying to accomplish. For example, you might
say:

> "Wow, this is interesting. We both agree that there is a
> problem and we've developed quite a few different solu-
> tions. Before we force ourselves to select one we might not
> be happy with, let's review what we know about the
> problem and see if that will help us choose."

Deadlock Breaker 4: Limit the Scope of the Problem

Negotiations occasionally break down because the players are trying
to do too much at one time. Each part of the problem might be easy
to solve, but the parts together are too much to deal with in one big
chunk.

You can get out of the "big problem" syndrome by breaking the
problem into smaller parts and dealing with each in turn. Say something like this:

> "You know, we may be trying to do too much at once.
> Let's try breaking this problem into smaller parts, and see
> if we can solve them one at a time."

If the other side agrees, see how many separate issues you can divide
the big problem into and try tackling them one at a time.

Deadlock Breaker 5: Increase the Scope of the Problem

This is the opposite of Deadlock Breaker 4 and is particularly useful when all of the solutions that come to mind are fine, in and of themselves, but they have a negative impact on other aspects you hadn't planned to discuss. When you run into a situation like that, try saying this:

> "We have looked at several solutions and each of them would have worked if it weren't for _____ [*the outside factor*]. Maybe we need to look at a bigger picture. This problem might just go away. What can we do about _____ [*the outside factor*]?"

Deadlock Breaker 6: Take a Break

Problem solving is hard work, and negotiators' creativity plummets when they get tired. Getting away from the table for a while will make it easier to find fresh approaches. A lunch break, coffee break, or short recess is often sufficient. Longer breaks are helpful when time permits.

Deadlock Breaker 7: State the Other Side's Case

People often talk past one another, especially when they are busy defending their own positions. After a while, the negotiation turns into a debate, with each player arguing for her own position and listening only for points that will bolster it.

You can get out of the debate trap by taking time to state the other side's case to the best of your ability. Break out by saying something like this:

> "We've been arguing over this point for nearly an hour.
> Let me make sure I understand you correctly."

Then paraphrase the other's position as accurately and neutrally as possible.

Over the years, many people have told us that they are afraid to try this approach because it seems like giving up. We disagree. We have never seen this tactic backfire. Rather, when you try it, you may see these results:

- The other player is impressed by your open-mindedness and responds in kind.
- Hearing you state his position, the other player may realize that he is being unreasonable and back off.
- Misunderstandings are eliminated and agreement is reached quickly.

Deadlock Breaker 8: Search for Common Interests

After a while, debate forces people to focus on points that separate them rather than on the interests they have in common. This is a natural result of disagreement, but it often makes the sides appear further apart that they really are. Break out of this trap by taking time to list the things you have in common. You might say something like this:

> "We have been arguing over this point so long that we may have lost sight of what we're trying to accomplish. Let's turn things around and see what we have in common that will help us find a solution."

Then suggest a few points that you have in common, and let the other party do the same.

Deadlock Breaker 9: Seek Additional Input

Occasionally negotiations grind to a halt because both sides have run out of ideas. This is a good time to seek additional input: a third party to add fresh ideas, new material to bring to the table, or trained mediators to reshape the negotiation process. The additional input may suggest possibilities that will resolve the deadlock.

Deadlock Breaker 10: Focus on Areas of Agreement

The most frustrating negotiations we have watched were those that broke down over a single point after the participants had resolved so many other issues. This happens more often than you might suspect because many people avoid the most difficult issues as long as possible. As the sides slowly realize that they have a real problem on their hands, tension grows because they understand that hours, days, or even weeks of hard work may go out the window over this final sticking point. Worse, because the final point is so important to them, the ability to compromise or create innovative solutions diminishes as the volume rises.

Managing this situation is one of the most challenging tasks you may face as a negotiator. We deal with it by reminding ourselves and the other side how much we have already accomplished. Here is a typical example:

> "When we started last week, there were seventeen areas of disagreement. Along with everything else, we have agreed on salary levels, benefit packages, and a uniform grievance procedure. With all that behind us, don't you think we can find a way to deal with the question of performance bonuses?"

Dealing With Those Who Refuse to Follow the Plan

Earlier, we noted that not all negotiators follow the natural order. Inexperienced negotiators break the order because they often don't know any better. They typically fall in line when you explain why the orderly process is important. But a few negotiators, a small handful, deliberately thwart orderly processes. Some are just too stubborn to try something new. Others—and these are the ones to watch out for—resist an orderly process because they hope to gain an advantage by throwing you off your stride.

Watch out for these negotiators, because they are often street smart and have some nasty tricks up their sleeves. Dealing with these hard cases will be one of your greatest challenges as a negotiator. Avoid them if you can. If you can't, remember the advice of a martial arts master:

"It doesn't matter how big or powerful your opponent is. All that matters is practicing your own art to perfection."

Here are the elements of your art to perfect if you have to deal with the hard cases:

1. *Expect the worst and prepare for it.* Negotiation with the hard cases is always a battle. It is an adversarial process, and you need to be hard and tough to hold your own. You may still find a win-win

solution, but it isn't likely. Concentrate on holding your own with the understanding that the results will be determined by the balance of strength and skill between you and your opponent. Standing up for yourself doesn't mean being rude or nasty. Just use the skills you have developed to state your own position and disagree without being disagreeable.

2. *Keep your cool.* The other player is counting on your agitation or discomfort. Some go to extremes to make the situation as uncomfortable as possible. They know that you are more likely to give in if you are uncomfortable and anxious to move on.

Are you familiar with the closing rooms some car dealers use? They are cramped, the colors are garish, and the furniture is uncomfortable. The rooms are like that not because the dealers can't afford better or have no decorating sense. Rather, the dealers know you are likely to overlook details of the contract if you are in a hurry to get out. They aren't the only ones using tricks like this.

Whenever you find yourself in a difficult position, get up and leave. Call time out, take a break, go for a walk, return phone calls— anything to relive the pressure and give yourself an opportunity to refocus on your own objectives.

3. *Don't waste your time or energy arguing about procedure.* Arguing about the procedure will tire you while your opponent remains relatively fresh because you carry the bulk of the load. Worse, arguments about procedure may distract you from more pressing matters, and you might even find yourself trading the order of discussion against a substantive issue.

Would you willingly pay $50,000 for the right to establish a relationship before discussing substantive issues? Not if you were in your right mind, but we saw one professional negotiator come perilously close before he realized what was happening.

4. *Don't let pressure from the other side force you to agree to anything before you understand the whole package.* Before the negotiation begins, make a list of the items to be decided and the critical issues. Then use the list at each stage of the negotiation to guide your thinking. During the negotiation itself, mark off items as they are discussed and clarified. Write down bits of information and tentative agreements as they come up, and don't accept any proposal until you have the whole picture. A quick glance at your checklist will show you what has been discussed and what remains to be decided. Whenever the other party presses you to agree to a particular point, postpone agreement by saying something like this:

"I see what you would like to do, but I'm still not sure about ———— [*any item that has yet to be discussed*]."

A Reminder

In this chapter, we have shown you how to structure any negotiation using the natural order as an ideal game plan. We've pinpointed what you need to accomplish at each step in the process and have introduced you to some tools and techniques that will help at every step. Exhibit 3-1 may help you remember the stages, your objectives, and the tools you can use.

This chapter has also presented some general approaches to conducting negotiation sessions and special tactics to help keep the process moving when the negotiation appears deadlocked. In addition, you've learned to play negotiation judo with the hard cases who won't go along with the natural order and how to make your anxiety work for you.

There is one other thing you should know about the negotiation process: Many negotiations are circular, and you wind up negotiating with the same player again and again. This is often true of negotia-

Exhibit 3-1. The basic game.

Step	Objectives	Tools
Relate	Establish or renew personal relationship with the other player.	Pay attention Conversation openers Renewal strategies Reciprocal disclosure
Explore	Identify underlying interests.	Open questions Probes Observations
Propose	Develop concrete proposal.	Homework First offers Checklist Closed questions
Agree	Agree on individual provisions and the entire agreement.	Disagree without being disagreeable Good reasons Graceful concessions

tions within an organization or with customers, clients, and suppliers you work with over a period of time. Think of the negotiation process as a great circle (Exhibit 3-2). Each new negotiation with the same party begins with a context created by the earlier negotiations.

★ YOUR MOVE

In recent months, your relationship with a key customer has deteriorated noticeably. You don't know of anything that could have caused a breach, but the signs are unmistakable. Phone conversations are crisp and to the point, with little or no social interaction, and written correspondence has become formal and impersonal. Hoping to find out what has gone wrong and rebuild your relationship, you have asked for and, after some hesitation, been granted an appointment scheduled for early afternoon.

Exhibit 3-2.   The negotiation cycle.

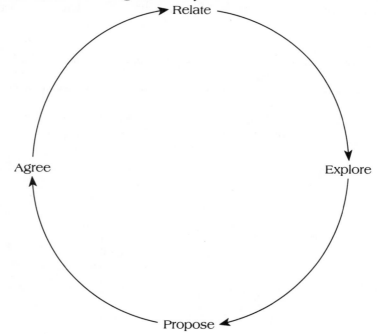

A secretary escorts you to a small conference room, where your customer is already seated at a small table with his back to the window. The only other chair in the room is on the opposite side of the table, and you will be facing directly into the sun if you sit down. What do you do?

One of your established clients has invited you to lunch to discuss some urgent business. You meet her at a nice restaurant—her choice—and spend a lot of time on social pleasantries while eating. Following the meal, she seems uncomfortable making the transition to business. What do you do?

You have been involved in a lengthy labor negotiation. Both sides have aired many concerns, but the discussions appear to be going nowhere. How can you get back on track?

ANALYSIS

Your customer has elected to use one of the oldest tricks in the book: deliberately putting you in an uncomfortable, subordinate position. You can counter the ploy by closing the blinds, moving the chair, or remaining standing. But in this instance, we think you should "fall" for the trick. Here's why: You know something is wrong but haven't been able to get your customer to explain what is bothering him. He has carefully staged this meeting and clearly wants to be in control. By letting him take charge, you may make him comfortable enough to talk about his concerns. If the negotiation moves on to other ground, then you can move to get the sun out of your eyes.

Although this is an established client, it looks as if something has happened to compromise your relationship, and you need to find out what. Since she is having difficulty making the transition to business matters, you should take the lead. Wait until the lunch dishes have been cleared; then lead with an open question. We'd say something like "That was a great lunch. Now, what did you want to discuss with me?" and wait for a response.

Don't make the mistake of leaping ahead to the proposal stage because too much remains to be clarified. Instead, use an internal summary to crystallize the issues. Say something like, "We've covered a lot of ground. Let me see if I understand your principal concerns," and list the two or three items that seem most important—on a flipchart if one is available. Then let the other side add to the list as needed. You can develop a proposal once you have a complete list of issues.

4

Getting Ready to Take the Field

Negotiations are frequently won or lost before the players even take the field. One side is so well prepared that the actual negotiation seems to be little more than an afterthought. Having prepared its game plan and anticipated the other side's moves, the winning team waltzes through the negotiation without strain or stress and barely breaks into a sweat, while the other side struggles just to stay in the game. That's why pregame planning is too important to be left to chance.

There are three reasons why pregame planning is so crucial:

1. *You can think more clearly before you're in the middle of the game.* Planning ahead helps you frame your position and craft your messages without undue pressure. It also gives you time to research the issues as well as the other side.
2. *Negotiation is an interactive process.* Your statements and actions don't stand by themselves. They are viewed in a context created by the other side's actions, and planning ahead reduces the chances you will be caught off guard. If you are blindsided, you can shift gears to other prepared materials while considering your response.
3. *It's difficult to carry your playbook onto the field with you.* Preparation gives you a chance to review critical skills, polish your presentation, and develop responses to probable countermoves by the other players. Our best advice: Plan hard and negotiate easy.

Most athletes use the off-season to develop their skills. Once the season begins, they concentrate on specific game plans. We recommend you do the same. Between negotiations, concentrate on skill

63

development, but focus on specific situations once you know one is coming.

This chapter will guide you through the process of preparing a specific game plan. In the pages ahead, you will find:

1. An overview of the negotiation process emphasizing the critical elements for which you must prepare
2. A worksheet of questions to help you prepare for any encounter
3. Guides for turning your preparation into specific actions and questions for each step of the negotiation process
4. Some tips for controlling anxiety that might limit your effectiveness

 GOOD TO KNOW

Preparing for a major negotiation is never easy, but there are some computer programs that will simplify the task. One of our favorites is *Art of Negotiating*, a remarkably easy-to-use program from Experience in Software. Once installed on your computer, the program prompts you to define the topic of negotiation; identify your objectives, issues and positions, needs and gambits, climates, and potential strategies. Along the way, you are encouraged to think about the other side's views, and a separate "idea screen" records ideas and options as they occur to you. When you are satisfied with your answers, the program generates a suggested agenda and proposes general approaches and specific actions that may be useful.

Art of Negotiating runs on IBM PCs and fully compatible computers, with at least 256K RAM, two 360K floppy disk drives or one 720K disk drive or a hard disk, and DOS 2.0 or higher. Available from Experience in Software, 2000 Hearst Avenue, Suite 202, Berkeley, California 94079-2176; (510) 644-0694 or (800) 678-7008.

Critical Elements to Prepare For

Exhibit 4-1 displays the critical elements in the negotiation process— the points for which you absolutely must prepare.

Exhibit 4-1. Critical elements in the negotiation process.

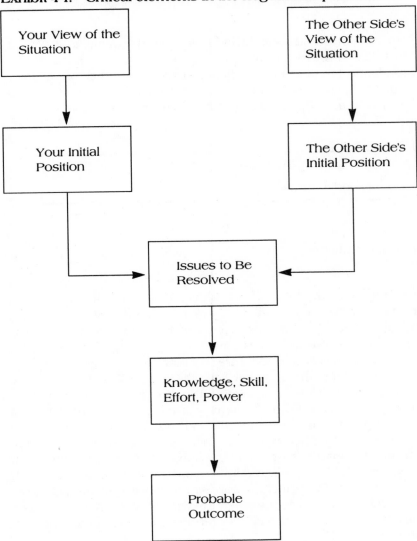

View of the Situation

Your view of the situation includes your needs, wants, and expectations. Thinking about what you want and how you might get it is the foundation for your initial position. Expect the other player to do some planning as well. Although he may not be as systematic as you, his view of the situation will give rise to his initial position.

"Luck favors the prepared mind."

Alexander Dumas

Initial Positions

Differences in the two initial positions determine the issues to be resolved. Typically you will find *perfect agreement* in some areas: The initial positions of both sides contain the same, or very similar, provisions. These nonissues pave the way for agreement in other areas. There will also be some areas of *perfect disagreement*. One player includes a "must have," while the other player lists the element as nonnegotiable. These are potential deal breakers, and they must be managed with great care. There may also be areas of *partial disagreement*. The initial positions are close but not in complete agreement. These areas may or may not be obstacles to agreement, depending on how far apart the sides are and how important the issues are to them. Finally, there will usually be some *potential issues*. We refer to these points as "potential" issues because they are mentioned by one side and overlooked by the other. They may become issues if there is disagreement, but they may also become nonissues if the other side agrees.

An example will help you distinguish issues, nonissues, and potential issues. Carol Smith has been assigned to buy a materials resources planning (MRP) system for her company. After considerable research, she has identified MultiSource as a supplier with which she could do business. The initial positions of the two players look like this:

Carol Smith	MultiSource
7 486DX33 PCs in an LAN configuration	5 486DX33 PCs in an LAN configuration
Level 4 MRP software	Level 3 MRP software
Installation and testing complete by January 1	Installation and testing complete by February 1
Free on-site maintenance for 1 year	Free on-site maintenance for 6 months
Significant performance penalty if system is out of service more than 10 hours per month	No stated position
Price not to exceed $130,000	Price $129,500
Bimonthly review of operating system software	No stated position
No stated position	Free on-site training for 20 employees
Free upgrades of operating system software for 1 year	No free upgrades of operating system software

Price is a nonissue; there is nearly perfect agreement here. Operating system software upgrades is an area of perfect disagreement, and there are also significant differences in the software level and duration of free on-site maintenance. Timing of installation and testing appears to be a minor issue, while potential issues include the performance penalty, bimonthly review of operating system software, and on-site training.

Once the issues have been identified, the knowledge, skill, and effort of the players are major factors in resolving the differences. The playing field is seldom level. Balance of power often determines how issues will be resolved. In rare cases, one side is so overwhelmingly powerful that all issues will be resolved in its favor. More often, power is divided between the two sides, and both teams are forced to be creative. Sometimes they find win-win solutions, sometimes they find compromises, and sometimes they walk away, unable to resolve the differences.

Power is always a factor in human interactions, and researchers have identified five types:

1. *Expert power* depends on knowledge and credibility. When you are seen to be an expert, others follow your recommendations because they respect your judgment.
2. *Personal power* is akin to charisma. People do what you want because they perceive you to be friendly, trustworthy, competent, and motivated by goodwill.
3. *Reward power* exists when you have the ability to give others something they want.
4. *Coercive power* is the ability to punish others who don't conform to your wishes.
5. *Legitimate power* exists when you hold a formal position that entitles you to give directions to others.

"The single most powerful tool for winning a negotiation is the ability to walk away from the table without a deal."

Harvey MacKay, *Swim With the Sharks Without Being Eaten Alive* (New York: William Morrow and Company, 1988), p. 103.

Although these forms of power are recognized as distinct, they often operate together. For example, an executive may have legitimate power based on the formal hierarchy, expert power based on experience and education, personal power, and both reward and coercive power.

You may find ways to capitalize on any and all of these sources of power, but *the ultimate power in negotiation is the ability to walk away without making a deal.* The more you need to make a deal, the less power you have. If you must make the deal, you are at the other player's mercy. Your power grows as your alternatives increase. If you have several attractive alternatives, you may be in almost total control. The fact that you don't need a particular deal means that you can pick and choose among those that are available and demand concessions from those who want to deal with you.

Consider Carol Brown's situation once more. If MultiSource is the only vendor she knows that can meet her needs, she is in a weak position. If there are several vendors who can come close, she is roughly equal in power. And if there is at least one other vendor that will conform to her exact requirements, she is in a very powerful position with regard to MultiSource.

In general terms, your relative power depends on the alternatives available. The more alternatives you have and the more attractive each is, the more powerful you are. There is an important object lesson here: You can create power for yourself by creating attractive alternatives. And you can also create the appearance of power by making it appear that you have at least one very attractive alternative.

The projected outcome is the final element in the preparation process. Based on your research and thinking, what is the most likely outcome? How are the issues most likely to be resolved? Your answer needs to be tentative because you have made assumptions about the other side's power and position, but making a guess is important. If you don't like the probable outcome, it's time to rethink your situation. You may also look ahead to Chapter 5 for strategies and tactics that will help you overcome the other side's advantages. Similarly, think about the other side's view of the probable outcome. If they like it, you have lots to work with. Conversely, if they don't like it, you need to be alert for tricks they may use to gain the upper hand.

The Pregame Worksheet

Understanding the critical points in the negotiation process paves the way for specific questions that will help you refine your thinking. In this section, we'll explain each of the questions and then assemble them in a worksheet you can copy and use to prepare for all of the negotiations you are likely to encounter. The first set of questions concerns your position:

- *What do I want?* Be as specific as possible when you answer this question. Remember, you should consider at least three factors: the substantive issues, your relationship with the other side, and when you need to reach agreement. It is a good idea to review Chapter 1 to make sure you understand each of these factors and their importance.

- *Why do I want each of these items?* The previous question gives rise to your position; this one points to your underlying interests. In fact, you may need to ask *Why?* several times, pushing your thinking even further to identify your specific needs, interests, and values. You can also divide the first question into component parts and ask why each of them is important to you. This process, called *fractionating,* is particularly important in complex negotiations and when you appear headed for lose-lose negotiations.

- *Who will be looking over my shoulder?* Most negotiations in professional contexts affect other people who may not participate but are sure to evaluate your work. Think about your boss, coworkers, subordinates, and other divisions or groups that will be affected by your work. You need to factor their needs and interests into your initial position and the projected outcome. Remember: If you fail to consider their reactions, you may face another less pleasant negotiation when you get back to your shop.

- *What should I propose?* Now is the time to develop your initial position. We suggest writing your answer in pencil because you may want to change it several times as you work through the rest of the process.

Having crafted your initial position, it's time to think about the other side's view of the situation:

- *Who is in a position to give me what I want?* Remember that your most immediate contacts may not have the authority to make a binding commitment, and you are wise to go straight to the top, or at least as far up the ladder as you can get.

"The first step in avoiding a trap is knowing that its there."

Frank Herbert, *Dune* (New York: Berkeley Publishing Company, 1965).

- *What does the other side want?* As you answer this question, be as specific as possible, and remember to think about their view of the substantive issues, relationship, and time frame.
- *Why does the other side want these items?* Getting beyond surface features will help you identify their interests. You can also fractionate their view as you did your own.
- *Who is looking over their shoulder?* In most cases, they answer to other people just the way you do. Knowing who will evaluate their work will help you identify hidden players on the other side and concerns that you might otherwise overlook.
- *How do they typically negotiate?* Think about their style: smooth and sophisticated, or rough and crude? looking for a win-win solution, or only interested in win-lose bargaining? flexible and creative, or rigid and demanding? Reflecting on style will also help you anticipate and prepare for dirty tricks.
- *What are they likely to ask for?* Your answer to this question will help you anticipate the other side's initial position. Since you are

making a guess, don't expect your answer to be perfectly accurate. However, the more you know about the other side, the closer you can come. Remember, these people have a history just as you do, and looking at how they have dealt with similar situations in the past will point you to their probable demands.

Now, look at both sides' initial positions. You can even create a table like the one we used comparing Carol Smith's position with MultiSource's:

- *What are the similarities and differences?* Your answer here will identify the issues for which you need to prepare. Look for areas of perfect agreement, areas of some disagreement, areas of perfect disagreement, and potential issues to which you must respond.

Looking at issues will help you anticipate the course of the negotiations as well as points of leverage you may use to persuade them:

- *What's in it for me if we do it their way? What's in it for them if we do it my way?* Your answers may suggest a win-win resolution of the issues, but there is no guarantee. You should also consider the balance of power.
- *What are my alternatives to making this deal? What are their alternatives to making this deal?* Your answers will tell you how powerful you are relative to the other side and help you project the most probable outcome.
- *How is each issue likely to be resolved?* When there are lots of issues, look at each one separately. You can also fractionate the issues, understanding that you may win a little and lose a little on each one.

Finally, it's time to evaluate the probable outcome:

- *Do I like the probable outcome?* If you don't, think about ways to change the situation or increase your power.
- *Will the other side like the probable outcome?* If the answer is yes, you may be able to accomplish more than you imagined and should consider expanding your initial position. If the answer is no, you need to be alert for tricks the other side may use to make the outcome more attractive for them.

(Text continues on page 76.)

Pregame Worksheet

Prepared _____ prior to negotiating with _____
            (date)   (other side)

about _____
                              (topic)

What do I want with regard to the substantive issues? _____

_____

Why? _____

_____

What do I want with regard to the relationship? _____

_____

Why? _____

_____

What time factors will affect my position? _____

_____

Why? _____

_____

Who will be looking over my shoulder? _____

_____

_____

What should I propose? _____

_____

_____

Who is in a position to give me what I want? _____

_____

_____

What does the other side want with regard to the substantive issues?

_____

_____

Why? _____

_____

What does the other side want with regard to the relationship? _____

_____

Why? _____

_____

What time factors will affect their position? _____

_____

Why? _____

_____

Who will be looking over their shoulder? _____

_____

_____

_____

(continues)

How do they typically negotiate? _____

_____

_____

_____

What are they likely to ask for? _____

_____

_____

_____

How do our initial positions compare? What are the similarities? The differences?

_____

_____

_____

_____

What's in it for me if we do it their way? _____

_____

_____

_____

_____

_____

_____

What's in it for them if we do it our way? _____

_____

_____

_____

What are my alternatives to making this deal? _____

_____

_____

_____

What are their alternatives to making this deal? _____

_____

_____

_____

How are the key issues likely to be resolved? _____

_____

_____

_____

_____

_____

_____

Do I like the probable outcome? _____

    If no, what can I do to change it? _____

_____

_____

_____

Will the other side like the probable outcome? _____

    If no, what are they likely to try to change it? _____

_____

_____

_____

OBJECT LESSON

Once the world's dominant computer manufacturer, IBM is in grave danger. It didn't respond to the emergence of personal computers quickly enough and allowed Microsoft's DOS to become the most common operating system. What few people know is that IBM made a "world beating miscalculation" in 1986 when it passed up the opportunity to buy DOS for just $75,000.

The lesson: Don't overlook the predictable long-term consequences of your actions.

From "Inside the Disaster at IBM," *Wall Street Journal* (August 16, 1993): B1.

Your answers to these questions will give you a more or less complete overview of the negotiation ahead. For your convenience, we've built these questions into the worksheet that starts on page 72; make as many copies as you like, and use one for each negotiation that matters to you. We usually use pencil with the worksheet because we've found that our answers change as we get more fully involved in preparation. And we've learned to look backward and try to change the situation whenever we are headed toward a losing negotiation.

Preparing Your Message

Completing the worksheet forced you to make a number of assumptions, or educated guesses, about the other side's view of the situation and approach to negotiation. We encouraged you to make your answers tentative because the early stages of a negotiation are your opportunity to learn more. Remember the REPA cycle described in Chapter 3? You can use it to take advantage of your preparation by developing a script or outline for the game to follow.

Step 1: Relate

Establishing a relationship with the other players is the first step in the negotiation process. Your preparation has helped you to identify the other party as well as their specific concerns and interests. Use this information to open the conversation in an informal, nonthreatening manner. Begin with socially acceptable small talk, or take advantage of your prior encounters by asking about mutual friends, family members, clubs or service organizations they belong to, current events, hobbies and recreational interests, vacations, or sports. In short, come prepared to start by talking about the things that interest the other side.

This is the time to do a lot of listening and observing. The other side's reactions to the warmup period will tell you a lot about their view of the negotiation. Are they open and friendly, or set for a confrontation? Their ability and willingness to engage in casual conversation will tell you if they are worried or anxious, working against a deadline, plan to take control of the negotiation, or want you to set the pace.

Step 2: Explore

The second stage of the negotiation is a time to check any assumptions you have made about their view of the situation. Exploring the general subject of the negotiation will help you be more specific about their underlying interests, and their view of the subject, relationship, and time factors. Although many of your questions will depend on the specific subject, here are several that work in most situations:

"Why do you think we should be meeting now?"
"Who is affected by the proposed changes?"
"How will you implement the new policy?"
"When would you like to close the deal?"
"What do you think is important here?"

Step 3: Propose

Now is the time to put a proposal on the table. You may take the lead by presenting your proposal, or you may wait for the other side. Here's how you might approach presenting your proposal:

"It looks as if we have some common interests. Here is what I had in mind."

Follow this statement by outlining the key features of your proposal or even handing out a copy if you have the proposal in writing.

If you decide to let the other side take the lead, listen attentively while they present their proposal. Use your own proposal as a checklist so you can see at a glance what they've included, how it compares to your initial position, and what they've added or left off.

Step 4: Agree

Reaching agreement is the final step in the negotiation process. Because so much will take place before you reach this point, it's hard to anticipate what you should say. However, summarizing the issues as you see them can be helpful. We like to open this stage by saying something like this:

> "We've covered a lot of ground. If I understand things correctly, we agree on [*list areas of agreement*], but we need to make decisions concerning [*list other key areas*]. Let's deal with the decisions one at a time. How about [*begin with the first area of disagreement*]?"

Making Your Anxiety Work for You

Are you anxious about getting into your first negotiation? Many people are—even the pros who have been through it a hundred times before. Here's why most people feel a little nervous when they step into the arena:

 **GOOD TO KNOW**

Communication scholars distinguish between two different kinds of anxiety. *State anxiety* is a natural response to challenging situations. A hand down from the fight-or-flight response of our ancestors, state anxiety includes a strong physiological response that promotes awareness, reduces reaction time, and increases physical and mental ability. *Trait anxiety* is a personality characteristic that reduces effectiveness. While almost everyone is afraid of public speaking, for example, a small percentage of the population suffers trait anxiety that makes it almost impossible for them to be effective in public situations. If our tips for dealing with anxiety don't help, you might suffer from trait anxiety and may want to seek professional assistance.

- The outcome is important. You wouldn't be negotiating if it weren't. (Remember, you can always walk away from the negotiations that don't matter.)
- Every negotiation is a performance. You are performing in front of the other negotiator(s), and other people—friends, colleagues, or people you represent—are going to evaluate your performance.
- The situation is likely to be unusual or out of the ordinary. Even if you have been through hundreds of negotiations before, each one has novel elements that will affect the outcome.

Don't let the anxiety throw you off your stride. It's a very natural reaction—in fact, it's nature's way of making sure you are on your toes. Anxiety isn't a problem unless it limits your ability to follow your plan.

Reading this chapter will probably do a lot to reduce your anxiety. After all, you now know what to expect at each step in the process. Knowing what to expect and knowing that you are prepared will do more than anything else to help you deal with the situation. However, here are some suggestions that you will find helpful:

- *Don't wait until the last minute.* Even if preparation requires only a few hours, spread them out over several days or weeks, and begin well ahead of time. Last-minute cramming wears you out and leaves you no time to reflect on or respond to anything you discovered in the process.
- *Don't make impossible demands on yourself.* In the best of all possible worlds, you might get everything you want all of the time. That seldom happens in the real world. There is nothing wrong with setting high goals; just make sure you don't set your expectations so high that you fail consistently.
- *Don't concentrate on failure.* Everyone stumbles from time to time, and it's good to learn from mistakes. But don't focus on them. Acknowledge your mistakes, learn from your errors, and move on to the next opportunity.
- *Don't use drugs or alcohol to calm your nerves.* You need to be alert and crisp to negotiate effectively. Drugs or alcohol may make you feel less tense, but they dull your senses when you most need them.
- *Check out the site ahead of time.* You would like to negotiate on your own turf, but that isn't always possible. Press for a neutral site, and check it out ahead of time. Knowing the lay of the

land will help you feel secure and give you a chance to locate time-out or cooling off spots.

- *Think of the negotiation as an extended conversation.* We emphasize *extended* because time pressure can put you at a disadvantage. Set aside as much time as you think appropriate for the negotiation, and plan to use all of it.

- *Feel free to take a break or call a time-out whenever you begin to feel pressured.* Some clever negotiators will try to gain an advantage by putting pressure on you, and walking away is the best way to escape.

- *Don't let yourself be outnumbered, physically or psychologically.* Nothing will do more to undermine your confidence than walking alone into a room full of hostile strangers. Whenever possible, find out how many players there are on the other side, and make sure you have as many with you. If the other side surprises you, call a time-out and reschedule the meeting on more favorable terms.

- *When you are part of a team, arrange for the other players to take you off the spot.* Over time, members of your team will develop an almost intuitive sense that alerts them to your need to step back. Before that sense develops, arrange some private signals to bring others to your aid.

- *Always use a checklist with all of the key issues.* The pressure of the contest makes it easy to overlook concerns, and using a check-list will help you make sure any proposal you agree to is complete and addresses all of the critical issues.

- *Practice all of the techniques we have reviewed in this chapter.* With practice, they will become second nature, and you will seldom be at a loss for what to do.

- *Remember your accomplishments as a negotiator.* As the old saying goes, "Nothing succeeds like success," and nothing will do more to restore your confidence than reviewing what you have already achieved.

Each of these suggestions will help you turn your anxiety into positive energy. With time you will add your own suggestions to the list.

Putting Your Plan Into Action

In this chapter, we've shown you how to think about the preparation process systematically and noted questions to ask at each stage of the process. Based on the initial analysis, we've also shown you how to craft your message at each stage and how to control the anxiety that naturally arises going into a critical negotiation.

We want to emphasize one point we made earlier: Projected outcomes can be favorable or unfavorable to you, favorable or unfavorable to the other side, favorable to both, or favorable to neither. These projections should alert you to both opportunities and threats. Exhibit 4-2 sets out the opportunities and threats in each of the four cases.

 YOUR MOVE

You have recently been appointed purchasing manager for a small manufacturing company. The company has a number of open contracts with local suppliers, and many orders are routinely processed without careful scrutiny. Reviewing the contracts, you find that one supplier appears to price its products at least 30 percent above the going market value. What do you do now?

You manage a distribution center for a respected national retail chain. Over the years, your company has built a reputation for quality service and products. However, you have noted an increasing number of complaints from store managers, who are your customers. They say that shipments are often incomplete and deliveries are sometimes late. Checking your records, you find that supplies and staffing are adequate and conclude that there must be an operational problem. To get a handle on the problem, you invite representatives of three well-established consulting firms to review the problem and make recommendations. All three agree that you have an operational problem, but they recommend very different approaches. One recommends a total quality management program and will charge $65,000 to create it, another recommends a customer service management/teamwork program costing $35,000, and the third recommends business process redesign (also known as "reengineering") for a price of $79,000. What do you do now?

 ANALYSIS

On the surface, this appears to be an easy problem to deal with. Most of us would be inclined to check prices to make sure they

Exhibit 4-2. Probable outcomes: opportunities and threats.

Your View of the Probable Outcome

		Favorable	Unfavorable
The Other Side's View of the Probable Outcome	Favorable	This can be a real win-win situation. Although you should be alert for unexpected features, you may be able to accomplish more than you anticipated.	You are headed for a loser. If the negotiation is relatively unimportant to you, think about walking away using the tactics discussed in Chapter I. On the other hand, if the negotiation is important to you, look ahead to Chapter 5 for strategies and tactics that may help you alter the projected outcome.
	Unfavorable	This promises to be a winner for you. However, the other side may anticipate this outcome, so be prepared with strategies and tactics. Protect yourself by anticipating their tricks and preparing to respond.	This looks like a lose-lose situation. Anticipate an unpleasant situation, especially if you allow the negotiation to become confrontational. However, you may find some innovative solutions if the other side is aware of the danger and willing to look for a mutually acceptable solution. Voice your concern early in the negotiation to test their response. If they are committed to conflict, hold your ground. If they signal flexibility, begin exploring ways to expand both sides' options.

really are higher than those of competitors, line up alternative suppliers, and then meet with the vendor to negotiate a better price. However, we suspect there is more here than meets the eye. There may be issues of quality, service, and delivery that are not apparent from price alone. And remember to see who is looking over your shoulder; someone in your company may have an interest in doing business with this supplier, and it would be a mistake to move before you know all the facts. Begin by talking to managers of departments that use the supplier's products; find out if they prefer this vendor, and why.

The greatest danger here is making a decision on price alone because you are comparing apples, oranges, and potatoes. The second proposal is dramatically less expensive than the others, but you don't yet know if it will solve the problem or have the benefits of the other proposals. We believe you need to start by finding out more about each of the proposed approaches. All three have been described in detail in relevant professional literature, and a brief search should help you find independent descriptions and assessments of the three approaches. As a starting point, here are some readings that will help you.

American Quality Foundation and Ernst & Young, *Best Practices Report: The International Quality Study* (1992); for additional information, contact Stephen L. Yearout, National Director, Operations and Quality Management, Ernst & Young, 1600 Huntington Building, Cleveland, Ohio 44115.

Tracy E. Benson, "Challenging Global Myths," *Industry Week* (October 7, 1992): 13–25.

David A. Garvin, "Competing on the Eight Dimensions of Quality," *Harvard Business Review* (November–December 1987): 101–108.

Michael Hammer, "Reengineering Work: Don't Automate, Obliterate," *Harvard Business Review* (July–August 1990): 104–112.

Peter F. Drucker, "The New Productivity Challenge," *Harvard Business Review* (November–December 1991): 69–79.

5

Strategy and Tactics in Advanced Games

Welcome to the advanced game. This is an important chapter, and we want to make sure you see it in perspective. Having mastered the basic game in Chapter 3 and the preparation process in Chapter 4, you already know everything—the tools, techniques, and approaches—you need to negotiate in the basic game. In fact, many successful negotiators never get beyond the basic game.

This chapter is for readers who want to play at a higher level—those who want to know more and do more. If you are satisfied with the basic game and like the projected outcome of most of your negotiations, at least for now, you don't need to study this chapter. In fact, we encourage you to set it aside until you are confident that you have mastered the basic game; everything we say here builds on the foundation established in Chapters 3 and 4.

Although you may want to skip this chapter for now, you will probably want to come back to it later. Virtually all of the participants in our seminars eventually want to look at this material. Few people are satisfied with playing a basic game, and their reasons for turning to advanced strategies and tactics will probably be your reasons as well. Here is what our clients and students have told us.

First, the greatest advantage of the basic game is also its greatest weakness. Playing a basic game will get you through most of the negotiations you ever face. However, the tools and techniques that are part of the basic game don't capture all the opportunities each situation offers. They may also leave you vulnerable to traps built into some situations. That's where advanced games come in. Advanced games employ strategies and tactics for capitalizing on the unique features of different situations you encounter.

Second, even if you are satisfied playing a basic game, there is a good chance that some of the people with whom you negotiate won't be. They have their eyes open for every nuance, wrinkle, or twist that

GOOD TO KNOW

Game theory is the formal study of strategy and strategic decision making. Many treatises on the subject are arcane and hard to read. An exception is this very readable account: Avinash Dixit and Barry Nalebuff, *Thinking Strategically* (New York: W. W. Norton & Company, 1991).

can give them an advantage. You can call these people sharks, cheats, con artists, or worse. But the thing they have in common is the desire to use anything and everything that gives them an edge. You may become their next victim if your play isn't at least as sophisticated as theirs.

Finally, the ease and simplicity of a basic game means that it won't hold your interest for long. Basic games get boring after a while. With a few successful negotiations under your belt, you may find yourself paraphrasing a popular song, "Is that all there is?" The answer is no, and this chapter will show you what more there is.

Here's what's waiting for you in this chapter:

1. Six rules to help refine your objectives—rules that will help you make the most of the opportunities that await you
2. Descriptions of advanced strategies that successful negotiators use
3. Ways to project yourself from "dirty tricks" that others may try to use against you

Six Unspoken Rules for Setting Objectives

You can never anticipate all of the specific situations you are likely to face, and no one can prepare you for all the games other people are likely to play. However, anyone who has watched professional negotiators work has to be impressed by their ability to respond to unique and interesting situations.

With years of experience, professional negotiators have developed some unspoken rules that guide their actions. We call these rules unspoken because they are seldom discussed and seldom shared with anyone other than close friends and colleagues. They are not original to us—far from it. All we have done is to write them down so you can learn and use them in your own negotiations.

Unspoken Rule 1: Always Look for Differences in What the Parties Want

This rule undergirds the thinking of skilled and sophisticated negotiators. It also reflects the special nature of the negotiation game.

Many of the games we learned to play as children are competitive; they force everyone to strive for the same thing—for example, scoring points, controlling territory, driving other players into bankruptcy, or being the first to cross the finish line.

Negotiations are more flexible, and more complex. In a negotiation, it is possible for different people to want different things. Well-negotiated settlements hinge on this fact, as some examples will show.

Many partnerships come to an end because the partners want different things. However, the differences can actually pave the way for an amicable settlement if the former partners don't let emotion interfere with good judgment. One gets the office products division, while the other gets the training and computer software units.

Another example is buying professional services. Although both buyer and seller are interested in price, they can often compromise to satisfy other interests. In exchange for a stable relationship and income, professionals may accept lower fees for their services. According to some recent reports, physicians reduce their fees by as much as 30 percent in exchange for the stability of long-term contracts with health care organizations.

One last example may be familiar. When there are two teenaged boys in the house, it's not uncommon to hear arguments about who gets the family car in the evening. When he got tired of listening to bickering about whose turn it was, a friend put an end to the argument by asking both boys why they wanted the car. The younger one wanted to show off for his friends; the older boy needed to go the library to work on a term paper. The solution satisfied both brothers: The older boy got to the library and the younger one's status was enhanced by the fact that he "had to" drive his brother to the library.

Unspoken Rule 2: Always Begin by Figuring Out Where You Are Starting From

Every negotiation takes place in a context created by earlier dealings. If you won big in the past, you can bet that the other person will be looking to get even. If you lost last time, you may be looking to get even, and the other party will probably be on guard.

Your reputation will affect other people's reactions as well. One of the craftiest negotiators we know goes out of his way to make people feel good about dealing with him. He will even give back concessions he has won in order to smooth future negotiations.

As important as the starting point is, it is just as important to think about how the outcome of a negotiation will affect future dealings. Goodwill or bad faith created in one negotiation comes to the table the next time two people negotiate. Goodwill makes it much easier to solve problems in the future; bad faith creates obstacles that limit possibilities down the road.

Unspoken Rule 3: Don't Expect Negotiation to Be "Fair"

Many of the games we play seduce us into believing negotiation should be fair. Designers go to great lengths to give everyone an equal chance of winning. Decisions are made by chance: the flip of a coin, the roll of the dice, or the draw of a card. Everyone is equal at the start: each has the same amount of money, the same number of pieces, or the same number of cards. Some games even use handicaps to make up for differences in the players' skills.

Making things fair in other games is intended to make them more entertaining. It's not much fun to play a board game you can't win, is it? But—and this is an important point to keep in mind— negotiation isn't about entertainment. It's serious business, and you often have to play with the hand you are dealt, even if the deck is stacked against you. Consider the relative plights of computer buyers and sellers over the past few years.

If you wanted to buy a personal computer a few years ago, there was no doubt who was powerful. You went to a small, crowded store where "techie speak" was the order of the day, and no one would translate for you. You took what they said you should at the price they dictated and hoped that technical support would be available when you needed help. Today the situation is largely reversed. Computer superstores have virtually driven the independent stores out of business. Dealers are anxious to answer your questions, even offering free classes to help you get up to speed. Rebates, discounts, and special software packages are common, and savvy buyers can often write their own deal.

Negotiation isn't fair because every negotiation takes place in a context created by many other forces. These forces combine to make some players more powerful than others. When you have the greater power, use it to promote your interests. When the other party has the greater power, look for ways to equalize the situation or minimize your disadvantage.

OBJECT LESSON

Carl Smith was offered a salary of $125,000 at an organization that normally paid executives at his level $150,000. He turned down the offer because it wasn't "fair." He later accepted a similar position with a salary of $110,000 at an organization that paid other executives at his level the same amount because it was "fair."

The lesson: Don't worry about what's fair. Instead, ask what's best for you.

Carl Smith is a fictitious case, but there is a growing body of evidence that executives make unwise decisions when they worry about fairness. For a review of this evidence, see Max Bazerman, *Judgment in Managerial Decision Making*, 3d ed. (New York: John Wiley, 1993).

Unspoken Rule 4: Look for Ways to Avoid Head-to-Head Competition

It's easy to spot rookies at the negotiation table: They come prepared to duke it out, no matter what the situation is. Many people think of negotiation as a game that's not over until one party emerges triumphant and victorious while the other slinks away, utterly defeated.

Certainly some negotiations are knockdown, drag-out affairs. But many are far more amiable. They leave both parties satisfied, looking forward to their next deal.

The difference between these two outcomes exists primarily in the minds of the players. If they expect a battle, they will find one. If they expect negotiation to be a cordial exchange, it will be. Once you begin looking for ways to satisfy everybody, there are all kinds of creative possibilities, as an example will show.

We often use a negotiation simulation to teach business students. A class is divided into three teams: one representing orange growers and two representing companies that use oranges. They are given time to study their companies, devise their strategies, and select a lead negotiator to bid for them. Nine times out of ten, only the orange growers get rich. The two buyer teams get locked into a bidding war, a war that ends only when one team goes broke and the other is so badly weakened that it cannot withstand the next round of negotiation.

In the tenth class, something wonderful happens: The students realize that everyone can win. One team wants orange pulp for juice, while the other team wants the rinds for another purpose. Even the growers can win when they negotiate beneficial delivery and payment schedules. These students learn that you open the way to win-win agreements by looking for ways that you can avoid head-to-head competition.

A simple trick will help you put this rule to work. When the other side begins making demands or insisting on particular features, don't say no or prepare a response. Instead, ask, "Why?" Keep asking until you find something you can do for the other side without compromising your own needs.

"Somehow, negotiating (has) become confused with machismo, as though the whole point is to outlast your opponent, to make him back down first. The point of negotiation is to reach an agreement that is mutually advantageous to both parties. To make it a contest of egos can only work against you."

Mark H. McCormack, *What They Don't Teach You at Harvard Business School* (New York: Bantam Books, 1984), p. 148.

Unspoken Rule Number 5: Don't Assume the Need to Compromise

Another common mistake is thinking that negotiation always leads to compromise. This view makes all negotiations seem like dealing with a street vendor. You know how it works: You see something you like and offer the vendor a low price, say $10. She smiles politely, shakes her head, and demands $20. After a bit of haggling, you settle on a price somewhere in the middle, around $15.

If you think street vendors are the only people who negotiate that way, consider the standard economist's interpretation. According to economists, every time you buy something, you have two prices in mind: the amount you want to spend and a reservation price, the highest amount you will spend. Sellers also have two prices in mind: the amount they want and the lowest amount they will accept, their reservation price. According to the economists, you can make a deal only if your reservation price is higher than the seller's reservation. In other words, making a deal depends on overlapping price ranges. Is it any wonder that economics is called the dismal science?

Dickering like that works only when price is the sole issue. The approach causes serious problems in more complex situations. Let's say you have to deal with the other person over and over again. From the first encounter, she knows you are a hard bargainer. The only way she can get more money is by demanding a higher price. So when you offer $8, she demands $22. You counter with a $6 opening bid the next time you meet, and so it goes.

That kind of dickering might be fun, but look what's happening: Every time you deal with one another, you get further apart, not closer together.

There's a second, more important, problem with that kind of bargaining. People who expect to compromise in the middle never take time to look for solutions that could help both. Buying from a street vendor is an unlikely example, but you might be willing to pay more in return for personalized delivery, and she might be willing to charge less in exchange for a stable customer. There are all kinds of possibilities. The point is that you will never find them as long as you limit your thinking to compromising.

Don't jump the gun here. We didn't say that you should always look for a win-win solution or that one is always desirable. We did say that you will never know if you don't look for more than compromise.

Unspoken Rule Number 6: Make Time Your Ally

This is one of the most fundamental rules skilled negotiators use. We're not talking about the time and effort invested in negotiation—

 GOOD TO KNOW

Some negotiators consciously use time to put you at a disadvantage. Setting a time limit is one of their favorite strategies. Sensing weakness or uncertainty, they will make a low-ball offer and pressure you to accept it by saying the offer is good only until they walk out that door. Our advice: Run, don't walk, out the door yourself.

the transactions costs mentioned earlier. We're concerned with dead-lines and other pressures that may force you to conclude a negotiation before the natural end of the process.

Time is never neutral; it always works to the advantage of the person who knows how to control it. When you have a strong position and aren't concerned about the other person's feelings, it makes sense to push for closure and get on with things. It also makes sense to hurry along when the situation could change to your disadvantage. There are also times when it makes sense to slow down. If you aren't sure of your position or think the other person is trying to take advantage of you, drag out the negotiations. You can set some intermediate objectives or focus attention on procedural matters. It makes sense to slow down when you have the weaker position but also when you want to build a relationship. Avoid pushing something down the other party's throat when you will have to deal with him in the future and want to lay the foundation for a good relationship.

These six unspoken rules will help you think your way through almost any negotiation. With experience, you will probably add your own rules to the list. When you do, we'd love to hear from you. Send us a note in care of the publisher so we can add them to our list.

Ten Common Negotiation Strategies

The basic game we've described is a straightforward application of a problem-solving strategy and the core of most successful negotia-tions, but it is only one commonly used strategy. The other strategies all have their own strengths and weaknesses as well.

Learning the other strategies should help you in two ways. First, you can add them to your own playbook to extend your repertoire. For example, if you don't care about maintaining a relationship with the other player and want to conclude a negotiation quickly, you might choose a power strategy, one that we will describe in this section.

Second, knowing these other strategies will help you understand some of the people with whom you negotiate. When you recognize their strategies, you will be able to figure out what they are trying to accomplish, how they plan to deal with you, and what you can do to protect yourself.

(T) GOOD TO KNOW

All of the strategies described here are in current use, but recent research shows that negotiators from different cultures use some more than others. For a useful summary, see Donald W. Hendon and Rebecca Angeles Hendon, *World Class Negotiating* (New York: John Wiley, 1990), pp. 226–228.

Strategy 1: Pseudo Problem Solving

Pseudo problem solving is one of the most deadly strategies, if you don't recognize it, and one of the easiest to counter when you realize what the other side is up to.

A negotiator using a pseudo problem-solving strategy will take great pains to make it look as if he is engaged in a problem-solving process. He says all the right things: "Let's lay our cards on the table and see what shakes out," "You are right; we do have a problem here. Let's see if we can find a fair and equitable solution," and "Why don't you begin by telling me what you need here?"

Sounds like a great start for a negotiation, right? Only if the other side is being honest with you; many are not. That's why we call this "pseudo" problem solving. With so much written about win-win negotiation in recent years, some sly players have found ways to make it work to their advantage. They know that they can learn a lot about you if they pretend to be engaged in a problem-solving process. Their goal is to get you to lay your cards on the table, disclosing your needs, interests, and concerns without telling you anything critical about themselves or their needs. In a short while, they know far more about the situation than you do, and they may turn this difference to their advantage.

People employing this strategy are often skilled communicators, and they use many of the communication skills we discussed in Chapter 3. They go out of their way to put you at ease. They show real interest in you, questioning and probing skillfully to keep you talking much of the time.

Fortunately, this strategy is relatively easy to counter, once you recognize it. Many of us have a kind of built-in radar detector. We get an uneasy feeling when something is wrong, even when we aren't sure what it is. Odds are good that your feeling is correct, but here is an easy way of making sure your intuition is on target. Once your radar detector goes off, take a mental break. Even better, try to get away from the table for a few minutes. Mentally list what you have told the other party about your needs and interests. Then compare your list to what you have learned about him. If you have told him far more about yourself than you have learned about him, you have good reason to take corrective action.

Here is the best way to correct the situation. The next time the other player asks you a question or probes for additional information, say something like this:

> "So far, we have talked a lot about my situation. Let me make sure I understand what you need."

Then ask a question and wait for the other person to answer. Be gentle and polite but firm. Don't say anything more about your needs and interests until you have heard from the other party. If he doesn't reciprocate, you know that you are swimming with sharks and can plan accordingly.

Strategy 2: Trade-Off

Someone using the trade-off strategy is willing to listen to any offer, no matter how outlandish, and will often make big concessions. You ask her to bring her price down $25,000, and she will bring it down at least $10,000; you ask her to improve quality controls by 50 percent and she will agree to improve it by 20 percent; you ask her to reduce interest rates by 7 percent and she will agree to a 3 percent reduction. Get the picture?

Someone using this strategy will meet you halfway on all your requests. That's another way of saying that everything is negotiable. Here's what you need to watch out for. Since she is so willing to make concessions, you might not notice three things:

1. She never comes quite halfway. Every concession is a little less than you had hoped for.
2. The initial demands are unreasonable—inflated initial prices, quality controls below industry standards, and interest rates above current market rates. As a result, even when she compromises, she still has an advantageous position.
3. Here is the real danger: She begins asking you to make concessions—a "fair trade," she may say, since she has already given up so much.

Why would someone use a strategy like this? She thinks she has a better knowledge of fair market values than you do and believes your desire to get a good deal will obscure your judgment. You might even try this strategy yourself if you don't care about maintaining a relationship with the other side, think you know more than she does, and know she is likely to be blinded by a "good deal."

To protect yourself, never enter into negotiation until you have done your homework. You should know the fair market value of anything you are negotiating *before* the negotiation begins. Then insist on using the fair market value, not the other party's inflated value, as the starting point for concessions. You might say something like this:

> "Before we get started, you should know I think your prices are out of line. Fair market value is _____ , and I'm going to consider that our starting point."

Whenever the other party comments on how much she has given up, remind her that you are starting at fair market value. She hasn't conceded anything, just brought her demands down to a reasonable starting point.

Strategy 3: Positioning for Acceptance

Some negotiators are skilled at describing their proposals in ways that encourage you to accept them. Their presentations are designed to short-circuit the reasoning process. Their topics address your most basic needs, their vocabulary taps into your personal makeup, and their delivery promotes trust and acceptance. These negotiators have carried the art of selling to a new level. Although they may appear to negotiate with you, most have already decided what they are going to "sell" you. There is little real problem solving and less give and take.

To us, use of this strategy implies little regard for the other party; it reduces the other player to an object to be manipulated by any means possible. We find that abhorrent and recommend that you never use such a strategy. However, you will run into some people who don't share our views. Here are some things you can do to protect yourself:

- Do your homework before the negotiation. Know reasonable prices, terms, and conditions.

- During the negotiation, write down the other party's arguments in *your own words*. Putting them on paper in your own words neutralizes many hidden devices.
- Press for definitions of loaded words: What is "unprecedented" demand? How long is a "limited time offer" good for? Which "international experts" endorse the product, and what makes them experts?
- Carry a checklist of points that need to be decided. Check items off as they are discussed; never enter into an agreement until all items have been resolved.
- When the other party is a particularly skilled persuader, take a break; get away from the table to review her arguments in private before signing off on any agreement.
- Give yourself a cooling-off period, at least twenty-four hours, before you sign any contract, agreement, or letter of intent.

GOOD TO KNOW

Two books will help you understand the psychology of influence: Robert B. Cialdini, *Influence* (New York: William Morrow and Company, 1984), and Genie Z. Laborde, *Influence With Integrity* (Palo Alto, Calif.: Science and Behavior Books, 1984).

Strategy 4: Power Play

Power is a key element in all negotiations. We have already encouraged you to use it when you have it and seek to neutralize it when the other player is stronger. It becomes a strategy when a party uses it to resolve disagreements. In extreme cases, all issues, disputes, or points of contention are resolved by appeal to power. The more powerful player may say, "That's the way it is because I say so." Here are some examples:

Manager to employee: "Do it my way, or I'll find someone who will!"

Manager to manager: "You'd better support me on this if you want my help in the future."

Supplier to customer: "You need to make a purchase now to stay on our preferred customer list."

Faced with this kind of pressure, the less powerful player may conclude, "I just can't do anything about it." But you can counter this strategy. Begin with an understanding of power strategies:

1. Perception is as important as reality. You have power if the other party thinks you do. Conversely, if the other party doesn't recognize your power, it has little value in negotiation.
2. Power comes from many sources: expertise (power based on knowledge), status (power based on formal recognition), authority (power based on rank and position), rewards and punishments (power based on control of valued resources), and influence (power based on the ability to persuade or shape the attitudes of others).
3. Use of power is governed by cultural standards. Many people in the United States resent being "manipulated" by powerful people. This is less true in other cultures.
4. Head-to-head confrontations are seldom effective uses of power. Some kinds of power erode with use and can be used up. More important, decisions based on power tend to be short-lived because the "losers" will seek to get back what they lost, and the "winners" must be on guard to protect their gains.

These four items help to explain when and how to use a power strategy, and what to do when someone uses one against you.

A power strategy can be used only when the following conditions exist:

- The other party recognizes and accepts your power, or you can create the appearance of power by referring to the sources of your power.
- You are not concerned about maintaining a relationship with someone who will resent the use of power.
- You are satisfied with a short-term victory.

When someone uses a power strategy against you, find out if the power is real or apparent. If it is not real, you can ignore it and proceed with your own strategy. If the power is real, try any of the following approaches:

- Ignore the power if the other player is not likely to follow through with the implied threats.

- Decide how important the issue is. If it is important enough, you may be willing to accept the consequences of the other's use of power and still pursue your own ends.
- Look for ways to reduce or minimize the other person's power.

Reducing or minimizing the other party's power is a time-consuming strategy, but it may be appropriate when the case is important to you. The key is finding alternatives to the negotiated agreement that will satisfy your needs. Find someone else to deal with, look for alternative sources of influence and support, or find an arrangement that will satisfy both you and the other party. You may even pursue all three approaches simultaneously.

Strategy 5: Fait Accompli

Fait accompli is Latin for "it is done." Literally, it means that the critical decisions have been made and cannot be reversed. In negotiation, this strategy is used to limit the range of discussion. Here are some typical examples:

"Salary ranges are set by Personnel. We can work on benefits packages, but we can't offer you a higher salary."

"I've already signed a contract with my supplier. As a result, I can't change delivery schedules or product features, but I might be able to adjust some prices."

"That's the best financing we could get at the time. We can always look for something better, but rewriting the contract will take time. You may have to go without your new car for a couple of weeks if we reopen the package."

Using this strategy effectively involves several considerations. There certainly are cases in which your hands are tied, but if you get a reputation for bluffing, you may lose the ability to use this strategy when it really matters. Limiting the scope of discussion is the primary reason to use this strategy. Use it when you don't want to discuss issues on which you are weak or vulnerable. To be effective, the limits must appear real, the consequences must appear realistic, and you must identify areas that remain open to discussion. You may even prepare to make concessions in other areas to mitigate the other party's anger or frustration.

Homework and knowledge are keys to your success when another party uses this strategy against you. If the limitations or consequences aren't realistic, challenge them. You might simply say:

> "Come on, Bob, you know Personnel will let you make exceptions."
> "Let's call your supplier and see what flexibility she has."
> "I'm sure the finance company will let me take the car now because they know I'm a good risk."

Even if the limits and consequences are realistic and the situation cannot be changed, feel free to make a big deal about them. Say something like, "That's a real problem for me—I don't know if we can live with that." You know you won't be able to change the situation, but you can wring greater concessions from the other party if you make it appear important. Finally, know your bottom line. If you can't live with the limits and consequences, walk away. Look for someone else to deal with.

Strategy 6: Funny Money

This strategy is an attempt to minimize the cost of a transaction. Here are some common examples:

> "This money isn't coming from your budget. It comes out of overhead and will never show up in your accounts."
> "Think about how often you will use this. It works out to less than a dollar a day. That isn't so much."
> "You are right. That does seem like a steep price. But, remember, it is all tax deductible. If you don't buy now, you will just end up paying more in taxes."

Use funny money whenever you think cost is likely to be an obstacle, but use it only if all other issues have been resolved or are likely to be resolved easily.

Protect yourself by doing your homework. Evaluate the offer by asking if the other party has accurately described the situation. Is it really just funny money? After the rebate or discount, is the total price really lower than the alternatives? If not, challenge the assumption, and wait for the other party to suggest an alternative. Be sure to look at the total price. Is it really so small? What about interest and carrying charges?

Strategy 7: Decoy

This red-herring strategy works by focusing attention on something other than the real or critical issue. In an extreme form, it may even be used to postpone discussion of the central issue until the other party is anxious to settle and will be more willing to make concessions, as these examples show:

- Knowing that salary and benefit concessions were the real issues, a union negotiator demanded job security. Eventually she was able to limit salary and benefit concessions in exchange for dropping the demand.
- In a weak rental market, an office building owner keeps rents artificially high by "helping" tenants calculate the cost of moving.
- An employee facing termination attempted to divert attention from her performance by attacking her superior, criticizing coworkers, and threatening to file a wrongful-termination suit.

Use a decoy when you have a weak position and when you think the other player will make concessions on the real issue in exchange for dropping the decoy. You may even play "bump and run," by introducing several decoys to keep the other side off balance.

Protecting yourself from a decoy is difficult because it is hard to see what's in the other player's mind. Your best defense is knowing what really matters to you. Think through the deal well ahead of time, and make a list of the items that are important to you. Don't make unreasonable concessions on these items, no matter what the other party says about side issues.

Strategy 8: Impasse

An impasse usually becomes apparent near the end of a negotiation. After everything else has been resolved, one player may say something like this:

> "We've worked so hard and resolved everything else. I'm afraid we will have to give up on the whole thing if you won't see me halfway on this."

Skillful players will even postpone the most critical issue to the tail end of a negotiation, making lots of concessions on less important points, and use an impasse to get their way on the most important feature.

Use this strategy when you have made so many concessions that further cuts will reduce the value of the deal below your bottom line, the point at which the deal has no value to you. You can also use it when the other party has no real alternatives or is likely to give up before you do.

Doing your homework is the best defense against this strategy. You can use the deadlock breakers discussed in Chapter 3, but the real key is knowing whether the other party really has reached his bottom line. This is also a good time to be patient. The other side may just hope you will give in first. Use your waiting time to create alternatives for yourself.

Strategy 9: Relationship Hostage

This strategy is based on a sound understanding of objectives in negotiation. As you know, three objectives are critical: the substantive issues, transaction costs, and maintaining important relationships. Someone using this strategy is attempting to balance relationship objectives against substantive issues and transaction costs.

Creative phrasing may disguise the trade, but this strategy is always expressed in phrases like these:

"If you really like me. . . ."
"If you value our friendship. . . ."
"Go along with me on this one, and. . . ."

This is a high-stakes strategy. The other side might easily decide that the substantive issues and transactions costs are more important than the relationship. However, you may still use it when you value the substantive issues and transactions costs more than the relationship. And you can use it when the relationship is more important than, or can be made to seem more important than, the substantive issues and transaction costs.

Being clear about what is happening is the first step in protecting yourself from this strategy. The other party really is threatening you! This is emotional blackmail. Saying no to her demands will damage or destroy the relationship. Control your emotions, and ask yourself the following questions:

- Just how important is this relationship?
- Are the substantive issues and transactions costs as important?

- Will she really sever our relationship?
- Who else can I deal with on this?
- Is there a way to preserve the relationship without giving in?

Your answers might not come easily, but they will help you determine the real value of the relationship so that you can make an objective decision. You may conclude that the relationship is worth saving, or you may conclude that the substantive issues, transaction costs, and your sense of self-worth justify calling the other party's bluff.

Strategy 10: Refusing to Negotiate

Many individuals and organizations use refusal as a strategy. They refuse to discuss the topic, skip meetings, avoid your phone calls, trash your letters, and walk away saying, "We've got nothing to talk about." More frustrating still is the institutional equivalent: "It's against our policy to discuss that."

Make no mistake, this is a powerful ploy. Use it yourself when you are not interested in negotiating because you have nothing to gain. You may also use it when your position is weak; the other party may give up and go away or settle for less when you finally decide to talk.

If you do it with tact, you can even use this strategy to increase the other party's stake in the negotiation. Think of a small child in a grocery store; the more her parent says no, the more the child wants the box of cookies and the more willing she is to settle for a smaller box. You can do the same thing by politely avoiding negotiation until the other side is really anxious.

When someone refuses to negotiate with you, you need to give him a reason to participate. That usually involves bringing outside influence to bear. The best way to do that depends on the situation. Here are some possibilities:

- Complain to the person's supervisor—in person if you can, in writing if you can't.
- Involve your supervisor or other company official.
- Write directly to the company's president or chief executive officer.
- Write to your congressman or representative.
- Sue. Use small claims court when appropriate, or retain an attorney to initiate a formal proceeding.
- Complain to a governmental agency or regulatory body.

- Complain to the Better Business Bureau.
- Have your credit card company withhold payment.
- Put scheduled payments in an escrow account until the matter is resolved.
- Complain to a professional association or board.
- Make the matter public through the media.
- Make a pest of yourself: call repeatedly, write regularly, picket the company's headquarters.

These are strong measures. Make sure that you don't violate any laws or contractual provisions. However, when all else fails, they may be your best way of getting attention.

Common Gambits: Protecting Yourself From Dirty Tricks

In addition to the general strategies, advanced negotiation games include specialized tactics. We use the word *tactic* to describe ways of dealing with particular problems at specific points within a negotiation. Other writers call them *gambits,* and define them as any effort to use knowledge of or assumptions about the negotiation process to gain an advantage. You may prefer calling them *dirty tricks.*

No matter what word you use, tactics differ from strategies in several ways. Strategies refer to the whole process of negotiation; tactics are used at specific points within a negotiation and may be used again and again within a single negotiation. Some negotiators have their favorites and resort to them whenever they want to break the flow or pattern of a negotiation. Other negotiators are more flexible. They try several tactics until they see what gets to the other party and then stick with the ones that work to their advantage.

Finally, tactics are likely to be used at particularly crucial points in the negotiation. Many negotiators use them when the other player is beginning to tire and may not recognize the trick. Gambits may also be used when deadlines approach or when the other side is flushed with success and may be most vulnerable. And some negotiators use them after the other player has made a public announcement and may not be able to back out of the deal.

We think such tricks distort the negotiation process and produce unstable agreements. Sooner or later, the person on the receiving end figures out what happened and sets out to get even. Unfortunately, we can't control the behavior of people around us. We know that many of them will use all the tricks in the book. Here is how we resolved our dilemma: We frown on the use of these tactics and discourage you from using them. At the same time, we would like to level the playing field, to help you protect yourself from the people who don't share our feelings.

Over time, we have found that the tactics are less effective if everyone knows what they are and is prepared to counter them. The remaining pages of this chapter describe nine of the most common gambits and show you how to protect yourself.

Common Gambit 1: The Printed Word

A written document may appear so formal and complete that people are less likely to question specific features. Additionally, critical terms and conditions may be tucked away, making them hard to find.

Some negotiators have learned to take advantage of the finished appearance of a contract. They may put it in front of you at the start of the negotiation. "It is," they say, "just a standard contract." Other negotiators wait until the close of negotiations and then volunteer to "take care of the work of drafting the agreement." A gracious offer? Perhaps. But don't be blinded by it. Remember, any contract can be rewritten, and it is usually advisable to have your attorney review a contract before you sign it. If the other player insists on using his draft, write on it at your first opportunity so it will have to be retyped no matter what.

Common Gambit 2: The Higher Authority

Higher authority is typically used near the end of a long and tiring negotiation. When you think all of the critical issues have been resolved and agreement has been reached, the other player will say something like this: "That's great. Now let me see if my boss will go along." What he is really trying to do is get further concessions from you. Having negotiated the best deal he could get, he is putting it on hold, and you may find yourself negotiating all over again. This time, however, you will be in a weaker position because the wrangling begins with the concessions you have already made.

When someone uses higher authority on you, try these responses:

- *Anticipate the tactic.* Begin by asking, "Do you have the authority for this deal?" Don't negotiate with the other party unless the answer is yes.

- *Turn the tables.* Say, "That's a good idea. I'll check with my boss too."
- *Set a deadline.* Say, "All right, but I need an answer by 6 P.M."
- *Call the other person's bluff by naming the tactic.* You can even sound humorous: "You aren't really going to try to use higher authority on me? I thought that gambit went out with the Eisenhower administration."

Common Gambit 3: Splitting the Difference

This tactic is also called nibbling because the other party is trying to nibble on your half. After each compromise, the other player suggests a further compromise. It sounds like this: "You know, we're so close to a deal, why don't we just split the difference?" The danger is that each split takes from you and gives to her.

Counter this tactic in these ways:

- *Reopen other issues.* Say, "Okay, but let's look at the whole package. We also need to split the difference on. . . ."
- *Refuse to play the game.* Say that another split is unacceptable, and begin to walk away. You will be surprised how many times the other person will back off.
- *Shift the burden.* Propose a split that takes from the other party.
- *Name the tactic.* "How long are you going to keep nibbling on my half?"

Common Gambit 4: Good Guy–Bad Guy

This is a classic tactic used by negotiating teams. One plays the good guy, voicing your position, expressing your interests, and supporting you; the other plays the bad guy, arguing, criticizing, and making things difficult. The danger is that they will throw you off your stride, each getting something of value from you. The good guy gets you to disclose your needs and interests but can't make a commitment. The bad guy keeps pounding on you and proposing agreements that work to her team's advantage.

Here are some ways to counter this tactic:

- Refuse to negotiate when you are outnumbered.
- Deal with only one of the other players. It doesn't matter which, but separating them will help you keep your balance.
- Get your own bad guy—somebody to do the dirty work for your side.

- Force them to reach agreement before presenting their positions to you. You might say, "It looks as if you haven't made up your own minds. Let's meet again when you have come to agreement."
- Publicly associate the two: "I know he speaks for both of you, and I'm going to take what he says as your position."
- Name the tactic. You can make a joke out of it, but force them to come clean before you get back to business. Our favorite response is, "You do the best good guy–bad guy routine I've seen in quite a while, but I'm not going to play anymore."

Common Gambit 5: Excessive Demands

Some negotiators begin by making large demands, hoping that you will compromise with them—a compromise that always works to their advantage. This is similar to the trade-off strategy (Strategy 2) but is likely to show up every time a decision is made. It sounds like this: "We can talk all you like, but I'm not going to accept anything less than the price I started with," or, "I don't care what you say. I'm not going to your plant unless you agree to pay my travel expenses."

This is neither a pleasant nor a sophisticated tactic, but you can deal with it:

- Do enough research so you know realistic values before the negotiation begins.
- Create alternatives to agreement that will increase your power and ability to walk away.
- Point out that the other person is being consistently unreasonable: "You have said the same thing about every issue. Aren't you getting a little tired of making big demands?"
- Walk away and close the negotiation when you lose patience. Even if you only create the appearance of withdrawing, the other party will be forced to back off to keep the negotiation alive.

Common Gambit 6: Take It or Leave It

This is another unsophisticated and unattractive tactic. It is similar to refusing to negotiate but may be used repetitively through a negotiation. Every decision and every turning point is met by unwavering resistance. "My way or the highway" is a recurrent challenge and leaves you few alternatives. Here are some of the best:

- Refuse to negotiate under these conditions. Say, "You've taken such a firm stand that we aren't making any headway. I guess we have to give up." Then prepare to walk away. The other player will back off if there is any real hope of agreement.
- Develop alternatives that give you power by satisfying your needs elsewhere.
- Remind the other person of the competition: "If you won't compromise with me, I guess I'll have to deal with Sue. She has a lot more flexibility, and we're already close to a deal."

Common Gambit 7: Take Away

This clever tactic works by making a proposal, agreeing with your objections, and then withdrawing the offer. Psychologically, it puts pressure on you to demand the best regardless of price. Here is an example: After explaining the features of a top-of-the-line computer, the salesperson listens to your response and says, "You may be right; perhaps you don't need state-of-the-art features. Let's look at some less advanced, older models." If you aren't careful, you may find yourself arguing that you really do need a top-of-the-line computer and signing a contract before you know what's happened: You've been put in the position of arguing the salesperson's case for her.

Defeat this tactic by doing your homework; know what you need and want before you get the pitch. The key is making your own decision and a price-performance graph; the one described in Chapter 7 is the best way to clarify the alternatives. If you are feeling mischievous, agree with the "take" and watch the salesperson try to recover. You may not get a better deal, but it's fun to play with the pros occasionally.

Common Gambit 8: Puppy Dog Close

This tactic is named after a gambit sometimes used by unscrupulous pet store owners. Seeing a child looking at a dog and trying to answer her parents' objections to getting a pet, the salesperson may step in and say, "The best way to find out if she will take care of the dog is to try it out. Why don't you take the dog home over the weekend? You can always bring him back on Monday." If you have ever tried to separate a child from her pet after a few days, you understand why so few puppies come back on Monday.

This is a particularly difficult tactic to counter, but you have some good options:

- Refuse to accept the "gracious" offer. Know whether you want the pet before taking it home.
- Be sure to get return provisions in writing. Watch out for restocking charges, depreciation allowances, and repair fees.
- Ask for a remedy other than returning the product—perhaps a price reduction or other services.
- Do your homework. Know what the item is worth before you agree to a trial period.

Common Gambit 9: Blaming or Shifting the Burden

This final tactic is transparent when you know how to recognize it. The other player will stretch out the negotiation, making you invest lots of time and effort in the process. Then, when you are largely committed to making the deal, he will start demanding concessions on particular points. When you resist, he says, "You know, we've invested so much effort in this deal, I'm surprised you would wreck it by objecting to this provision."

You've heard this one before if you grew up in a family where parents used guilt to control their children. The only question now is whether you can still be treated as a child. You have two options:

1. Name the tactic, making a joke about it if you like, but indicating that it is not an acceptable way to deal with you: "Not even my mother uses guilt like that anymore."
2. Turn the tables on the other player: "You're right, we have invested a lot of effort in this deal. Now you are raising so many objections that I'm not sure you really want to make a deal."

As always, your research will prepare you to walk away. You should know alternative ways of satisfying your needs and the costs and benefits of each. When the deal is over the limit, say "thanks for your help," and head for the door. You can bet the other player will find a way to accommodate you if he really wants to reach agreement.

★ YOUR MOVE

Driving home from work, you see a garage sale sign and notice an antique dining room table in the middle of the garage. Your family has been talking about buying some antiques, and this one looks ideal.

You stop to look and find the table is authentic and appears to be in good condition. While you are looking, a very pleasant woman comes out of the house and asks if she can help you. You say you are interested in buying the table but think the price is too high. The haggling is fun, and you do get some concessions. She will have her son deliver and reassemble the set, and she will "throw in" a vase that looks "just right on the table." Finally, you agree to pay her asking price and she says, "Oh good. Now let me see if it's okay with my husband." What now?

 ## ANALYSIS

You see what's happening, don't you? This is no amateur you are dealing with, and she has just sprung the trap—two of them, in fact. She has drawn out the negotiation to build your commitment and then hit you with higher authority. Now that you recognize the traps, you know the options. Here's what one of the authors said in this situation: "You know, that's a good idea. May I use your phone? My wife knows a lot more about antiques than I do, and I'd like her to see it before I spend this much money." The prospect of a hard-bargaining wife saying no changed things considerably: The need to check with her husband disappeared, the son promised to deliver the table at our convenience, and the price went down while another vase was added to the package.

6

Etiquette

We often begin seminars by asking participants to write a brief description of a recent negotiation in which they have been involved. At first we were surprised to see how much space people devoted to describing their opponents. We've learned a lot since we began using the exercise, and we are no longer surprised.

Other players are what makes the game interesting and challenging. In fact, you couldn't even play if there weren't someone sitting on the other side of the table. The other player can make the game interesting and challenging—or boring and dull. The other player can make the game pleasant, one you enjoy playing and would like to play again soon. She can also make you feel awkward and anxious. In fact, more than a few negotiators have walked away swearing never to "deal with that _____ again." If you have never experienced that feeling, brace yourself! You will before your career as a negotiator is over.

Here is something you should recognize if you haven't already thought about it: Other people experience the same sorts of feelings when they negotiate with you. They may walk away feeling pleased and satisifed, even if they "lost" on the substantive issues, or, they may walk away glad to be done with the ordeal, even if they "won" on the substantive issues. Your conduct makes the difference in their experience. In fact, winning and losing often have little to do with the other players' feelings after a negotiation. If you conduct yourself appropriately, they will conclude the negotiation feeling that you are a "good person," a person they look forward to dealing with again. If you conduct yourself inappropriately, they may have very different feelings and avoid dealing with you in the future.

Etiquette is the study of personal conduct and its effect on other players. Few people realize how their conduct affects negotiation. The overwhelming majority of negotiations take place between people who come from the same culture. They share an understanding of the process and adhere to the same code of conduct. As a result, common sense is an adequate guide in most situations. Since both sides share the same rules, the negotiation process seems natural and uncomplicated.

Common sense is a good guide most of the time, but two specialized cases call for advanced skills. One arises when you negotiate with someone from another culture. When the other side does not share your understanding of the process, behaviors that are normal to you may be wholly unacceptable to him. Moreover, the smallest nuance in your conduct can have dramatic consequences because it has specific meaning to the other player, a meaning that you neither intended nor understood.

The second case arises when you deal with someone who knows your culture and shares your understanding but chooses to break the rules to gain personal advantage. These are the bad guys. They do whatever they can to get the upper hand. They know that their conduct may make you uncomfortable, and they hope that you will overlook critical points or rush to close, even if you have to do it on their terms.

This chapter introduces some advanced skills that will help you cope with these special situations. In the pages ahead, you will learn:

1. How cultural differences affect the game
2. What do watch for in playing with someone from a different culture
3. How you can learn the rules employed by other cultures
4. How to spot the bad guys
5. Ten common approaches employed by the bad guys
6. How to counter their moves

Playing With Someone From a Different Culture

Every culture includes rules of conduct, the unwritten guides that people learn and use without conscious attention. We learn them as children; our parents and teachers guide us in dealing with other people until we can conduct ourselves in socially acceptable ways. Over time, these rules become second nature to us, and we don't even think about them. Here are some examples:

- Be on time for meetings.
- Don't embrace strangers.
- Control your emotions; don't express them openly in business contexts.

 **GOOD TO KNOW**

When doing business overseas, keep the following points in mind:

- Don't make comparisons with your own country, and don't criticize others' customs.
- Don't remark about "funny money" or appear incapable of dealing with local vendors. Learn the country's monetary system.
- Formal titles are very important; learn and use them.
- When you are planning an extended stay, have the reverse side of your business card printed in the language of the country, and double-check it for accuracy.
- Avoid idiomatic expressions; they are often meaningless when translated.

We accept these rules—aspects of our own culture—without question. Following them makes it easy to interact with people who share them. However, they make dealing with people from other cultures chancy.

Seven Key Differences

Cultures are almost infinitely variable, but research is beginning to paint a clear picture of the essential elements. There are seven critical areas in which the ground rules change from culture to culture. Being alert to these differences will help you avoid blunders:

1. *The purpose of the negotiation session.* North Americans think of the negotiation session as a time to hash out issues and come to agreement. As a result, positions are open to debate, and all assertions are subject to challenge. Both sides are expected to produce evidence when needed, and claims are seen to be little more than efforts to win support.

In contrast, many other cultures view the negotiation session as a time to present decisions made elsewhere. Positions are fixed, at least for the duration of the session, and assertions are accepted as representatives of carefully crafted stances. They should not be challenged or criticized, and producing evidence is inappropriate. In extreme cases, North Americans' habit of debating the issues is considered offensive, and challenging assertions is a sign of disrespect. While the North Americans debate issues, the other side may well be working to save face.

2. *The significance of time.* North Americans think that time is money and expect everyone to be on time. Negotiations are expected to move quickly and cleanly to an explicit conclusion that marks the end of the session. In contrast, people from many other cultures do not assign such great significance to time. They arrive when they arrive, usually within an hour or two of the appointed time. Being late is the norm in many cultures that expect negotiations to proceed at their own natural, unhurried pace. They may view negotiations in terms of their long-term consequences and think nothing of spending days or even weeks building a relationship. Critical issues are brought to the table only when both sides are comfortable with procedural matters. As a result, foreign negotiators often see North Americans as pushy and abrupt.

3. *Personal conduct and interaction.* These matters are highly variable in North America, and appropriate conduct depends on the relationship between the players. Physical contact, including handshakes, slaps on back, and even hugs, is appropriate when greeting old friends. In contrast, executives from overseas are often much more reserved. Their rules of conduct are more formal and less subject to change with the nature of the relationship. In extreme cases, formal conduct shows respect, and failure to employ prescribed forms is a sign of incompetence or disrespect.

4. *Expression of emotions.* Open expression is generally frowned upon in the United States because our culture tells us that emotion is not part of business. People from many other countries take a different view. They believe emotions are important, but acceptable forms of expression vary widely. In some countries, they are expressed with decorum, in limited or controlled ways. In still other cultures, failure to express emotions openly is a sign of distrust. In either case, North Americans' unwillingness to deal with emotions is often a barrier to successful negotiation.

5. *The use of power and prestige.* North American culture values equality and fairness, and appeals to power or prestige are considered inappropriate. In other countries, power and prestige are accepted as essential components of the negotiation process. High-stature players are selected for the negotiating team, and they expect to meet with others of equal status. Adding to the North Americans' dilemma, open references to power and prestige are typically used primarily to correct errors of those who fail to acknowledge rank and status.

6. *The use of physical space.* North Americans value privacy and carefully guard their personal space. Invasions of space signal power plays and attempted intimidation. In other cultures, space has less value, and players are accustomed to getting close, often leaning over one another's shoulders. In extreme cases, failure to get close indicates lack of trust, and North Americans' efforts to preserve their space give the impression that they are cold and unreachable.

7. *The statement of positions, needs, and interests.* North Americans value frankness and directness, and people are inclined to put it all on the table. In other cultures, such directness is not valued and is often viewed as a lack of sophistication. Your counterparts expect you to infer their positions from your knowledge and their veiled references. While we like to focus on "essential issues," the potential deal breakers, others use guarded and indirect references to potentially difficult topics. In extreme cases, explicit discussion of critical issues is taken as a sign of incompetence. It may even suggest that the North American negotiator is not sophisticated enough to employ appropriate rituals.

Learning New Ground Rules

As you can see, even the most basic ground rules differ widely from culture to culture. As you become involved in more and more negotiations with people from different cultures, you need to be able to understand what their rules are; then you can use them when you choose or explicitly acknowledge and demonstrate respect for them when appropriate. One way to test whether a rule exists is to try to break it. If you get punished or receive negative reactions, the rule you just tested did exist. Unfortunately, it's often difficult to recover when you have broken a rule. Even if negotiation isn't terminated, you may find yourself dealing from a subordinate, one-down position.

Here are six less threatening ways to learn new ground rules:

1. *Be knowledgeable and informed.* There are many good books on specific cultures. Some give you the flavor of the culture and specific tips on doing business with its representatives. Whenever you deal with someone from a culture you don't know well, set aside time to go to the library and read up on the country.
2. *Review your experiences with members of the culture.* You can also learn from friends and associates who have dealt with repre-

sentatives of the culture, and an "Americanized" member of the culture can often be a valuable guide. The next way is to watch carefully, with your eyes, your heart, and your ears. In general, people are more likely to give themselves away in their nonverbal behavior than in the words they choose. When in doubt, follow their lead.

3. *Let the other player lead.* Many will take your hesitation as a sign of respect, and your observations will help you find socially acceptable—to them—ways of addressing your concerns.

4. Whenever possible, *use preliminary correspondence to establish the ground rules.* Use the list of key differences we just provided to guide your inquiries so you won't be caught off guard at your first meeting.

5. *Ask the other side how they prefer to conduct the session.* Many will appreciate your sensitivity and interest, and do whatever they can to accommodate you.

6. *Take advantage of consultants, agents, and educators when you prepare for major negotiations.* Their services aren't free, but you can easily save more than you spend by avoiding even a single blunder.

Playing With the Bad Guys

Negotiating with someone from another culture is interesting and challenging because there is a lot to learn. The same is true of dealing with the bad guys, but for a different reason. Whereas someone from another culture doesn't know or use our rules, the bad guys take advantage of the rules by breaking them whenever it suits their purpose. Here is an example from a recent labor negotiation:

> The senior member of one team arrived forty-five minutes late and took a seat near the middle of the closed room. Leaning back in his chair and putting his feet on the table, he lit one of the largest cigars we have ever seen. After a minute or two, he exhaled a cloud of thick blue smoke and opened the session by saying, "Let's get this _____ session on the road." Members of both teams reacted with shock and disgust. Confronted with such grossly inappropriate conduct, their nonverbal behavior screamed, "He can't do that; what's wrong with him?"

This is typical bad guy behavior. By breaking rules, he has put others off guard and changed the pace of negotiation. Notice that the other players' reactions have played right into his hands: They are worrying about his behavior, and he has taken charge of the negotiation. The longer they remain distracted, the more he can do to settle the issues on his terms.

Not all bad guys are so outrageous, but all have learned to gain advantage by breaking the rules. They are often among the least pleasant people to deal with, but deal with them you must. The key is understanding that they are neither socially inept nor inconsiderate. Their behavior is often deliberate and well polished; it helps them get what they want. And they stop doing it when it no longer produces results they value. Sound simple? It is once you know what to look for. Getting angry doesn't help; in fact, it often hurts you. The more rattled you get, the greater is their advantage. You can right the situation by breaking the link between behavior and rewards.

As you can imagine, it's not difficult to spot the bad guys. There are lots of them out there, both journeymen and apprentices, and subtlety isn't their strong suit. Sometimes it's difficult to distinguish real bad guys from people who are merely inept, but our method of dealing with them doesn't require fine distinctions. Whenever another player's behavior makes it difficult for you to concentrate on the task at hand, treat this person as a bad guy.

Ten Common Bad Guy Behaviors

With time and experience, you will learn to spot the bad guys and counter their moves. To help you get started, the following paragraphs describe some that have gotten our attention over the years:

1. *The tough guy.* He is often physically large and thinks nothing of intimidating you. Invading your physical space is one of his favorite tricks, and he may also resort to explicit threats. What's in it for him? Just like all other bad guys, he knows that he can get an advantage by distracting you. As long as you focus on his behavior, he is in charge and can shape the negotiation to his advantage.

2. *The slow, indecisive player.* She doesn't do anything quickly; even ordering lunch is an ordeal because she questions every detail. These players literally bore you to death. They hope that you will eventually concede even major points just to get the negotiation concluded so you can get on with other business.

3. *The blowhard.* His behavior is characterized by telling long, irrelevant stories. He is constantly sidetracking discussions, interjecting unrelated comments, and focusing on things that are irrelevant. What's the point of this behavior? After a while, you become inattentive—maybe even tune him out. Then he can slip in important provisions without your critical scrutiny. In extreme cases, his behavior creates a situation in which critical decisions are made at the tail end of the process without careful attention to detail.

4. *The time bomb.* She's easy to spot: red face, rigid posture, flexed muscles—ready for an explosion. Confronted with a potential explosion, most people back off. They may make inappropriate concessions, soften their positions, or avoid sensitive issues just to sidestep the anticipated explosion.

5. *The emotional cripple.* His whimpering, crying, whining, lack of eye contact, and head-down posture display his inability to deal with the issues. The danger is that you will take pity on him. You may conclude that he has enough problems already and avoid pushing your position or demanding appropriate concessions. If you doubt that his behavior is an act, watch his disposition change once the negotiation is concluded.

6. *The vulgar or offensive negotiator.* He often resorts to inappropriate language, tells off-color stories, dresses inappropriately, displays poor personal hygiene, or resorts to bodily noises to make you uncomfortable. As your discomfort grows, your attention to details diminishes and you may eventually sign anything just to escape.

"Never get in a spraying contest with a skunk."

G. F. Reidenbaugh, Associate Dean (retired), Syracuse University, telling a young teacher how to deal with a difficult colleague

---

7. *The Archie Bunker imitator.* Archie was a consummate bad guy in many respects. Recall the early years of the television show ("All in the Family"), and you'll understand what we mean. This bad guy has strong opinions on every subject and expresses them freely. His behavior makes it difficult to establish a relationship or explore mutual interests because there is no neutral subject. He expresses himself with vigor on every subject, and it's often impossible to

distinguish between real concerns and tangential issues. What does he get out of this behavior? He learns far more about you than you learn about him.

8. *The unceasingly critical opponent.* The key to recognizing her is that she is never satisfied. She criticizes everything: you, your organization, the proposed agreement, even the meeting room and coffee service. Intentional or not, her behavior makes the situation uncomfortable for everyone. If you aren't careful, you'll find yourself trying to accommodate her rather than concentrating on the key issues to be negotiated.

9. *The poor host.* Negotiating on his turf is a nightmare because he does whatever he can to make you uncomfortable. Pay attention to the setting or you may find yourself sitting in an undersized or broken chair. The poor host may blow smoke in your face, seat you staring into the sun, or set the thermostat to an uncomfortable temperature. He gets more than the pleasure of watching you squirm; he knows that discomfort distracts you from the issues at hand and increases his chances of getting a favorable deal.

10. *The one-track debater.* She comes back to the same issue again and again. She won't let anything else be discussed, and her behavior may deadlock the entire negotiation. Don't mistake her behavior for simple ineptitude. She is putting extreme pressure on you to make concessions on the specific issue. However, you will soon notice that once that issue is resolved in her favor, she adopts the same posture for the next.

This list of candidates for the hall of shame reflects our experiences and those of our clients. You will probably encounter all of them, as well as some we haven't met. Fortunately, the same strategy will help you counter all of them.

Countering the Bad Guys Without Becoming One of Them

We have seen negotiators respond to bad guys in a variety of ways. Some ignore the behavior and hope that it will go away. Others adopt bad guy behaviors themselves, and the negotiation quickly becomes a contest of bad manners. Neither approach is adequate. Ignoring the behavior takes effort and may play into the other side's hands. And becoming a bad guy yourself makes it all the more difficult to reach a mutually acceptable solution.

GOOD TO KNOW

Dealing with the bad guys is particularly difficult when someone else is watching. Does it help to go on the attack? Probably not. Recent research has focused on observers' reactions to verbal attacks questioning the character, competence, background, appearance, and motives of the other person. The finding: People who launch attacks are viewed as aggressive and less competent, and with fewer valid arguments, than those who have a more temperate approach.

From Dominic A. Infante et al., "Initiating and Reciprocating Verbal Aggression: Effects on Credibility and Credited Valid Arguments," *Communication Studies* 43 (Fall 1992): 182–190.

We prefer a direct but not frontal assault on the behaviors by outthinking the bad guys. Here's how we do it whenever we feel uncomfortable:

1. We take a break and identify the source of our distress.
2. We describe the behavior as precisely as possible, often writing a concise description of it.
3. We identify our own reactions and the reward the bad guy is getting.
4. We list a couple of ways to break the link between their behavior and the reward.
5. When we return to the session, we try the approaches one at a time until we find one that works.

Two examples show our thinking process and some of the approaches we might use:

Behavior: **She complains about everything. She began by criticizing the room and morning coffee service, and she hasn't stopped since.**

| *My reactions:* | I've tried to accommodate her by switching rooms and ordering more coffee. I've spent more time trying to make her comfortable than arguing for my own position. |

| *Her reward:* | She has succeeded in distracting me from the key issues. If this continues, she will get her way because I'm too distracted to build my own case. |
| *Possible countermoves:* | • I can shift the debate by asking her to present her position.
• I can use a two-column technique and get her to list both good and bad features of the proposal.
• I can confront the behavior by using an asserting message. |

Behavior: **He has manipulated the situation to put me at a disadvantage: I'm staring into the sun and can't read or focus on him.**

My reactions:	I've tried to live with the situation and haven't done anything to change the setting.
His reward:	He has the psychological advantage. I am in a subordinate position and can't make my case effectively.
Possible countermoves:	• I can close the blinds. • I can use delaying tactics until the sun moves. • I can reschedule the meeting on neutral turf.

Whenever you find yourself dealing with a bad guy, take a break and reflect on the situation to identify your reactions, the reward of the other party, and possible countermoves.

YOUR MOVE

Your boss is an absolute tyrant: He has to have the last word on everything and never admits he is wrong, even when it is obvious to everyone else. Staff meetings are an ordeal. He lectures everyone and gives you your marching orders for the week. Whenever someone objects, he humiliates and belittles the person. You keep losing good staff, and those who have stayed are afraid to speak up. What can you do to get him to change his ways?

You are preparing for an important overseas trip to meet the key executives of a firm with which you would like to do business. Correspondence and telephone discussions have been encouraging, and you expect to sign a contract while there. What do you do when one of the key executives calls and volunteers to make hotel reservations for you?

Meeting a foreign business person for the first time, you begin by exchanging business cards. What do you do with the card you are handed? Here are four options:

1. Slip the card in your pocket and continue talking.
2. Read the card, then put it in your pocket, and continue the conversation.
3. Study the card for a moment or two. Then set it on the table in front of you before resuming the conversation.
4. Hold the card carefully in both hands and study it intently until the other player looks up. Then place the card on the table in front of you before resuming the conversation.

ANALYSIS

Most people confronted by a problem boss make the mistake of focusing on his behavior. You can make more progress by focusing on your own. Take a few minutes to identify his behaviors, your reactions, and his rewards. Then think about ways you might change your own behavior. Here are some suggestions:

- Meet with your boss in private and explain how his behavior affects you. He may be unaware of how he is viewed. He might even ask you to help him change.
- Accept the fact that your boss isn't going to change, and find a way to live with his behavior.
- Find a new boss.

This is a gracious offer, and you would be treated well if you accepted. However, there is danger here, and we recommend that you decline graciously. Why? Once they know how long you are planning to stay, your hosts may control the agenda to their advantage. Worse, some foreign hosts have been known to bug their guests' rooms. We suggest you have a knowledgeable travel agent make your reservations. It's also advisable to get an open-return-date airline ticket so you can stay as long as necessary.

There is more going on here than you might expect. Responses 1 and 2 are the most common North American practices, but both may offend your new associate. Title and status are often more important in other cultures than in ours. The business card is considered an extension of the person, and the way you handle it demonstrates your respect, or lack of it, for the other person. We recommend the fourth response for formal encounters such as a business meeting. The third is acceptable for more casual encounters.

7

Buying and Selling

Buying and selling are like other negotiations. You can use all of the strategies and tactics we have discussed, and you can rely on a basic game whenever you want. However, buying and selling are unique in one respect: You are involved in them far more often than any other form of negotiation. For example, you may get a new job and negotiate salary and benefits packages once every five years. That's about the national average. In contrast, you buy and sell every day of your life. In fact, you are probably involved in many transactions every day. Some are relatively minor, and you may not pay much attention to them: buying a newspaper, grocery shopping, exchanging goods and services with friends and colleagues. Other transactions are major events: buying a new office building, negotiating a line of credit, purchasing consulting services, contracting with a new client. These are important purchases, and they can have dramatic effects on your career because everyone affected by the deal will be looking over your shoulder.

Because transactions are such a large part of our lives, our clients and students have asked for specialized buying and selling tools. Assembling the tools wasn't difficult; professionals in many fields have long concentrated on buying and selling. Researchers have studied their techniques, and practitioners and scholars alike have generously shared their experiences and insights with us.

Price is the focal point in many transactions. People usually begin by asking something like, "How much will it cost? or "What will you give me for it?" We believe this is often the wrong way to start a negotiation, but we will follow common practice and start with it too. Here's what you will find in this chapter:

1. Observations to help you put price in proper perspective, whether you are buying or selling
2. Sources of competitive intelligence to help you give proper attention to price and other factors relevant to the transaction

3. Strategies to help you emphasize price when it works to your advantage and deemphasize it when it doesn't
4. Tactics to boost the price when you are selling and lower the price when you are buying

The Significance of Price

Price is a significant factor in many transactions. Mass merchandisers advertise "everyday low prices," offer "best price guarantees," and promise to "double the difference" if you find a lower price. Auto manufacturers price their vehicles "thousands less than the competition" and regularly offer rebates. Home buyers and sellers haggle for hours over prices, and even professional services are frequently discounted for "our best clients."

It's nice to get a bargain, but attention to price frequently obscures other important concerns. A decade ago, a survey of corporate purchasing agents identified eleven critical buying factors. Price ranked sixth in importance. Updating this list to reflect current conditions brings the number to more than twenty items:

availability and quality of technical support services	literature and manuals
prompt delivery	stability of supply
quick response to customer needs	design assistance
product quality	predictable transaction costs
supplier reputation	ideas for future products
price	accuracy of order entry
completeness of product line	accuracy of invoices
quality of sales representatives	ease of order entry process
extension of credit	completeness of orders
personal relationships	responsiveness of sales force
	responsiveness to special requests
	ease of product returns

Whether you are buying or selling, this list should alert you to items that are at least as important as price, in even the most commonplace transactions. If you disagree, consider buying a daily newspaper. Timeliness is a primary factor here. Even a 50 percent discount does little to make up for consistently late delivery.

This list has a noteworthy implication for sellers: Know what the buyer values. An organization recently surveyed its customers to see what they considered important. Of eleven items, the top two were accuracy of order entry and accuracy of invoices. Surprisingly, the organization's own sales force rated these items fourth and sixth. In fact, the sales force and customer rankings agreed on the relative importance of only one item.

Over time, you should be able to categorize your customers according to their long-term purchasing behavior. Most fit into one of the following categories:

- Loyal buyers who buy from you year after year regardless of offers and promotions
- Technical features buyers who look for bells and whistles and state-of-the-art products
- Best-deal buyers who always go for the best deal available at the time, often driving hard bargains to show others how well they are doing
- Creative buyers who tell you what they want in the way of products, services, and prices
- Fringes buyers who look for fringe benefits—added goods and services thrown in
- Chiselers, who constantly negotiate for price reductions
- Nuts-and-bolts buyers who select packages offering the best value
- "CYA" buyers who worry about others' reactions and always go to name vendors

Reviewing this classification, you should recognize that people don't simply buy products or services; they buy complex packages of goods and services that satisfy their needs. Price may be a dominant factor for some, an important factor for others, and a minor consideration for still others. Effective selling requires recognizing what's important to each customer and positioning your product accordingly. For some, you package all of the features and benefits you can, knowing that price is a minor concern; for others, you strip away all of the features and benefits to sell a minimum product at the lowest possible price; and for many you find a point between these two extremes.

The same notion is important to buyers as well. Most merchants don't simply sell products or services; they sell bundles of products and services calculated to satisfy your needs. Their calculations aren't always perfect, and some make very different assumptions about what you want and need. Some produce large and complex bundles designed to provide a high level of service and a comprehensive product. Others provide minimal service, even self-service, and a stripped-down product. Many fall between these extremes.

Whether you are buying or selling, competitive intelligence—finding out as much as you can about the other party—is critical. As a buyer, your objective is to identify the potential sellers who come closest to satisfying your particular needs. As a seller, your objective is to learn what your customers need or want and how you can package your goods and services to get the highest possible return.

 GOOD TO KNOW

Purchasing consulting services is a critical transaction, and many executives have been disappointed by the results. Research indicates that at least some of the blame rests with the executives rather than the consultants. Eveleen Bingham, a consultant based in London, has identified the behaviors that cause much of the difficulty: the *carper*, an executive who complains about everything; the *disappearing act*, senior executives who won't take time to meet with the consultant once a contract is signed; the *switcheroo*, changing the contact person for an ongoing project; the *foolish miser*, organizations that cut corners when implementing a new program; and the *amnesiac*, executives who don't remember why they hired the consultant in the first place and constantly change the assignment.

From Anne G. Perkins, "Consultants: Bemoaning the Rotten Client," *Harvard Business Review* (July–August 1993): 11.

Gaining Competitive Intelligence

Understanding what the other party wants and needs will help you create a total package that satisfies your needs and theirs, and it will help you respond to their proposals and structure your own.

A few years ago, we recommended that negotiators learn everything they could about the other party. Today, there are so many sources of information that we suggest a more modest goal: Learn as much as you can in the time you have available. Your search cannot be perfect; the transaction opportunity may be long past if you try to learn everything that could affect a deal.

Here's what we think you should try to learn before you enter into a transaction:

- The combination of goods and services that will best satisfy your needs
- A reasonable price for that combination
- Who is most likely to satisfy your needs
- Your alternatives

That's a formidable list. Fortunately, so much information is readily available that you should have little difficulty compiling answers to these questions. You probably won't spend much time on these when you are engaged in trivial transactions and no time at all when making routine purchases. On the other hand, you may spend weeks and months researching major transactions. Many purchases will fall somewhere between these extremes. The choice is yours. The more you know, the more you may accomplish in the negotiation. But research is a time-consuming process and can easily consume more effort than it is worth.

Some sources of competitive intelligence help both buyers and sellers. Other forms have primary value to sellers or buyers. The following lists are intended to direct you to sources of information that will assist you.

Sources of Competitive Intelligence for Buyers and Sellers

- The library. Use this invaluable resource to look for recent books, magazines, buyers' guides, pamphlets, and directories of commercial organizations. Reference librarians can often point you to sources of information.
- Relevant professional literature. Product reviews, research, and usability studies, as well as articles describing companies, industries, and current developments, can often add a great deal to your knowledge.
- Personal and professional contacts, friends, and colleagues. Once they know what you are looking for, many will share their knowledge, experiences, and recommendations. While you are at it, don't forget people you've met at society meetings, courses, and seminars.
- Public records. Realtors regularly tap public records of recent

transactions to help price individual properties. You can do the same or rely on appropriate professionals.

- Computer information services. This resource offers an increasing number of price guides, including some based on recent transactions. They also permit you to search recent news stories and announcements, bankruptcy notices, liens, and judgments reflecting other players' ability to fulfill their obligations.
- Your stockbroker or financial adviser. Company and industry reports contain a wealth of information. You can also gain access to these documents through search services and databases available at better public libraries.

Methods for Sellers to Gain Competitive Intelligence

- Act like a customer, calling, visiting, or ordering from your competitors. If you are too well known to get unbiased information, send an associate.
- Use your customer contacts. Many will be glad to tell you what competitors are offering and how their products and services differ from yours.
- Talk to former customers—those who have stopped doing business with you. Find out who they deal with now, how their current suppliers differ from your organization, and what you can do to recover their accounts.
- Follow up all inquiries. Call back a month or so after the inquiry to find out if they are still in the market. If they've decided not to buy, find out why and what you can do to sway their decision. And, if they've bought from someone else, find out who and why.
- Talk to colleagues and competitors. Your colleagues may be willing to share information when they get something in return from you. Some may even share their best ideas and alert you to potential difficulties. Competitors are usually more guarded, but they often appreciate opportunities to gloat and may tell you more than they should about their best deals.

Methods for Buyers to Gain Competitive Intelligence

- Comparison shopping is a must. Visit, call, or write several vendors, and use what you learn to identify key features of their products and services, differences in product or service bundles, service policies and guarantees, and prices.

- Review your own records of major transactions. From whom did you buy in the past? What inducements did the sellers offer? How well did they service your account? Were inquiries handled in an appropriate professional manner?
- Take advantage of reader service cards in magazines to order information. You will be surprised by the amount of information you can accumulate for the price of a stamp. In addition to brochures, many vendors send product reviews, samples, and special promotional information.
- Read *Consumer Reports* and related magazines—essential sources when you are buying personal items. Look for annual buying guides, and search through back issues at the library.
- Contact recent customers. A list provided by the seller may be carefully screened, but you can still compare these customers' needs to your own. Even here, well-planned questions and probes may reveal problems the seller doesn't know about.

GOOD TO KNOW

Buying and selling a business are complicated because it is difficult to establish a fair market value. Do you choose *market value*, the total price at which a company's stocks and bonds trade in financial markets? *liquidation value*, the price at which the company's assets would be sold if it were broken up? *net present value*, the discounted value of free cash flow after interest and taxes plus the value of depreciation? or the *known value of comparable companies*? Each of these approaches has advantages and limitations. Negotiations typically center on differences in the approaches preferred by buyers and sellers.

For further information, see Robert C. Higgins, *Analysis for Financial Management*, 2d ed. (Homewood, Ill.: Irwin, 1989), chap. 9.

- Review company and industry reports by brokerage firms, as well as other records indicative of the vendor's financial condition, if guarantees and continued service are important. A company in financial difficulty may not be able to make good on its promises, even when well intentioned and written into the contract.
- Talk to professionals who service the industry. Bankers, lawyers, brokers, and consultants may be willing to advise you at

little or no cost. Even healthy fees may be recovered by your savings on major purchases and investments.

Transaction Strategies

Once you have completed gathering competitive intelligence, it's time to begin making strategic decisions. The most critical strategic decision concerns the extent to which you let price dominate the negotiation. Sometimes you want to focus on price alone. This is typically the case with commodity products. At other times, you want price to be one of several considerations. For example, price may be important but linked to timeliness of delivery. There are even times when you would like price to be the least significant issue. When you are buying a computer system to run your business, for example, price is considerably less important than ease of installation, the ability of your employees to operate the system, reliability over time, and prompt service.

We use the term *price consciousness* to refer to the relative importance of price in any transaction. Both buyers and sellers should be alert for ways to manipulate price consciousness. Buyers typically try to increase price consciousness when competing products are nearly identical and when they are filling a short-term need. They aim to reduce price consciousness when they want additional features or services and when the quoted price is attractive and they would like to get concessions elsewhere. Sellers, on the other hand, work to increase price consciousness when they are the price leader. When competitors offer lower prices, sellers generally struggle to reduce price consciousness by emphasizing other features and benefits. The following strategies will help you increase and decrease price consciousness.

Strategies to Increase Price Consciousness

Since many people begin negotiations focusing on price, you seldom need to increase sensitivity to it. However, sellers may want to concentrate on it when their price is better than the competitors'. Buyers may want to increase price sensitivity when price is the dominant unresolved issue and they would like to get further concessions. The following strategies often work here:

• *Use charts and graphs.* Differences in price show dramatically on a graph. Simple line graphs placing the least expensive products on the left and progressively more expensive products to the right show the range, and bar graphs make differences in price unmistakable.

A price-performance chart is particularly useful when different product characteristics obscure differences in price. For example, there are so many personal computers on the market that it's easy to get confused. Prices range from a few hundred dollars to more than $10,000, and performance variables include processor, speed, memory size, and hard disc capacity. Graphing the differences with prices on the vertical axis and performance on the horizontal axis shows the relative value of each product. Here is a simple example:

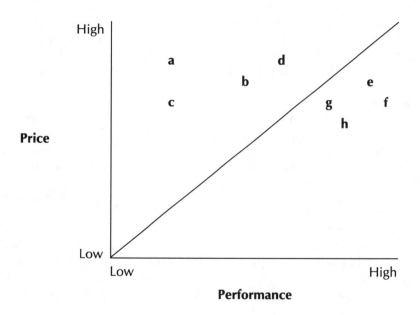

The diagonal line is a regression line, but there is no need to apply a complex formula. Simply draw a diagonal line with about as many items above it as below it. Items below the line are relatively good values at each price point; those above it are not. In this example, items e and g are good values, and f and h offer the highest level of performance for the price.

• *Reduce the perceived importance of making a deal.* Here's the thinking behind this strategy: The more important a deal is, the less attention people pay to price. They may even be forced to make a deal regardless of price. For example, a manufacturer recently paid an exorbitant price for computer chips that were in short supply. It faced losing a major customer if it couldn't deliver an order on time; the value of the customer's goodwill was greater than the cost of the chips. The converse is also true: When making the deal is unimportant, price emerges as a primary concern. A few months later, the same manufacturer was able to get a much better price because supply was abundant and it was not under pressure from a valued customer.

To increase the other person's perception of the importance of the deal, consider these three methods:

1. Create lots of alternatives and talk about them freely.
2. Appear inattentive and uninterested, frequently changing the subject and talking about irrelevant matters.
3. Postpone negotiation, arriving late for meetings, missing or rescheduling meetings, and getting called away from meetings.

Use these approaches with discretion. You don't want to offend the other side, and you don't want them to give up. You are ahead of the game while they are working to make the deal happen and your attention is elsewhere.

Strategies to Decrease Price Consciousness

There are many times when you will want price to be a minor or incidental feature. Sellers typically use this strategy when their price is higher than that of their competitors. Buyers use this strategy when they are satisfied with the price but want concessions on other issues. Here are some approaches to decrease price consciousness:

- *Emphasize the total package*—all of the goods and services included in the deal. Focus on features and benefits of the total package, and add to the bundle whenever price considerations are mentioned. For example, computer dealers often add software, training, network capability, central processing unit upgradability, and on-site services to sweeten the deal. This strategy works by making the total package so attractive that price seems small in comparison. Pushed to the limit, this package makes price an afterthought.
- *Get the product into the buyer's hands.* Let him work with it, get used to its features, and become convinced that it is better than

anything else he has used previously. Low introductory prices, lease-purchase arrangements, and trial periods are often designed to encourage customers to test products and services. The more the buyer is dazzled by the product, the less attention he will pay to the price. Your leverage increases enormously if the potential buyer becomes dependent on the product. And you can consistently raise prices if the cost of switching to another product exceeds the amount saved.

▪ *Focus on perceived quality.* Favorable reviews, news reports, and customer comments can be used to increase the perceived quality of your product or service. Add to these positive experiences the buyer has had with your other products or services, and you have a nearly unbeatable package. In fact, research indicates that world-class companies regularly command prices 30 percent above industry averages.

▪ *Guarantee satisfaction.* A properly worded guarantee reduces buyer anxieties and encourages her to focus on what she is getting rather than how much she is paying. We typically include the following provision in our consulting contracts:

> Your complete satisfaction with this project is our primary objective. If you are not wholly satisfied at any point, you may terminate this agreement, paying only for work completed, with no further obligation.

If none of your competitors offers a comparable guarantee, your position is even stronger.

▪ *Increase the perceived importance of making the deal.* The thinking here is that the buyer will pay less and less attention to price as the importance of the deal goes up. Here are four ways to implement this strategy:

1. Get the buyer to make a public statement or commitment to the deal. For example, announcing a tentative settlement or test-driving a new car over the weekend is a public statement that limits the buyer's flexibility.
2. Convince the buyer to buy quickly because this is a limited time offer, quantities are limited, or new models will be more expensive.
3. Apply pressure to the buyer by getting influential people to recommend or insist on the purchase.
4. Create a valued relationship with the buyer, a relationship that will have priority over price considerations.

Buying and Selling Tactics

Increasing and decreasing price consciousness are global strategies governing your entire approach to a transaction. There are also specialized tactics to handle prices. Thousands of dollars may be at stake even if you have reduced price consciousness. These tactics are even more useful when price is the primary issue.

Nine Tactics Sellers Use to Boost Price

Boosting prices generally works to the seller's advantage. After all, higher prices translate into increased margins and larger commissions. However, there are three factors to consider before you blindly set out to boost prices.

First, and foremost, the potential lifetime value of a customer is often greater than the gains from a one-time sale at an inflated price. When your product or service is one that customers may use repetitively, boosting the price is a poor idea because it reduces the chance of repeat business. The same is true when your customer is in a position to refer others to you.

Second, boosting price is a poor idea when it will adversely affect your public image. The damage done by taking advantage of a situation may linger for years, long after the short-term gains have been consumed.

Finally, many states have enacted consumer protection laws. Aimed to protect customers who have been "oversold," these laws generally give buyers a specific period of time during which they can repudiate any transaction.

With these qualifications in mind, here are nine tactics you can use to boost prices:

1. Make a first offer at the high end of the price range but imply flexibility. Flexibility keeps the other party from walking away, while the high initial point means that compromises will work in your favor.
2. When the other party is not particularly knowledgeable, let him make the first offer. There is a good chance that it will be high. You can refuse it if it isn't high, but the fact that it is the other party's offer makes it a credible starting point when you treat it seriously.
3. Politely refuse the other player's first offer and provide good reasons for saying no. The reasons adjust the other's mental

price range and give her a way to justify a higher price when reporting to interested third parties.

4. Whenever you are faced with an unacceptably low offer, make a counteroffer. Don't focus on price alone. Boost the price as much as possible while stripping away value-added features. You may be able to sell them later as extra cost options, and stripping them away makes it possible to reduce the apparent price without reducing your margin.

5. Increase the perceived value of the purchase by emphasizing special features and the unique bundle of goods and services.

6. Compare your price and product to the competition's. Your reasoning should note that your product is significantly better but your price is only slightly higher.

7. Promise the buyer something of value as an inducement to paying the higher price. Free advertising, referrals, discounts on other merchandise, and advance notice of sales and special offers are valuable to buyers but cost you little or nothing.

8. Increase the buyer's willingness to pay a higher price by showing several less attractive alternatives at the same price. The trick is to get the buyer to associate the proposed price with unsatisfactory items and understand that something of real value costs more. For example, realtors often show several unattractive properties before showing the one they expect to sell. A prospect might buy one of the less desirable properties, but the real purpose is to condition the buyer's mind to the higher price.

9. When cross-selling or preparing a package of goods and services, sell the most expensive item first. Timing is critical because items after the initial sale seem relatively inexpensive and are less likely to become the focal point for objections. For example, auto salespeople always push accessories after selling the car, and clothiers show shirts and ties after selling the suit.

Seventeen Tactics Buyers Use to Lower Price

Buyers typically aim to lower prices; anything that they save stays in the budget for other uses. Pushing for lower prices is a generally accepted practice in our culture and in most others. But even here, there are some limits to be aware of. Pushing too hard can damage your relationship with the seller, making subsequent negotiations more difficult. Success also has its price, especially if you get the price so low that the seller's ability and willingness to service your account is compromised. Finally, if you are too relentless, the seller may conclude that you are just playing a game and turn to other matters.

When all is said and done, however, it is still a good idea to test the seller's lower limit. Here are some tactics you can use:

1. Don't offend a seller by making an inappropriately low offer. Instead, have an acquaintance make an unreasonably low offer first. In comparison, your offer seems much more attractive, and there is no animosity directed toward you.

2. Always refuse the first offer. You know it isn't the other player's best offer, and you need time to find the real range.

3. Visibly flinch or react in some other way to show shock on hearing the other player's first offer. Your reaction will help recalibrate the other player's sense of value. If other people see the exchange, all the better because the seller then needs to impress them as well by making concessions.

4. Offer good reasons when refusing the first offer. The reasons give the other player something to work with and may help her justify the final price to another interested party.

5. Never close negotiations without making a counteroffer. Don't focus on price alone. Think also about stripping away value-added features that are of little interest to you and services that you can get elsewhere cheaper. There is a good chance that you will later get the buyer to add these items back into the package at no extra charge.

6. Compare a quoted price to competitors' prices. Your homework here is invaluable because it lets you evaluate each offer and demonstate knowledge of reasonable prices to the seller.

7. Simply ask for a better price. This tactic will often get you a better deal. Just ask, "What is the best price you can give me?"

8. Inquire about special discounts, promotions, and special rates. They may be available; you won't know if you don't ask.

9. Hesitate when you hear the other person's proposal. If you don't react immediately, he may think you are preparing to reject the offer and sweeten the deal before you make any requests.

10. Offer the other party something of value in return for price concessions. Stable relationships, continued business, referrals, and word-of-mouth advertising cost you little but may have considerable value to the seller. Coincidentally, some research shows that it costs five times as much for a seller to get a new customer as to keep an existing one, so you may have considerable leverage if you buy regularly.

11. Get offers and proposed prices in writing before you leave to think it over. For example, always get the salesperson's card and write prices on the back. Better still, have her write the prices for you and sign the card. If you don't find a better deal elsewhere, the written offer gives you leverage even if you return to find another salesperson on duty.

12. Always deal with someone who has the authority to give you a better deal. Part-time employees, junior clerks, and trainees seldom have authority to cut a deal and seldom benefit from bonuses.

13. After you have agreed to buy, ask for free services or accessories. In the favorable afterglow of a completed negotiation, the seller may give back things that he refused earlier. Perhaps not, but it never hurts to ask.

14. Never stay where the salesperson leaves you when he takes your offer to the sales manager for approval—a variation of the higher-authority gambit. Go look at a cheaper model. If another dealer is next door, step over and start looking at that competitor's product. You'll be surprised how quickly the salesperson gets back with an approved deal. Coincidentally, did you know that some sales managers are nicknamed "Mr. Otis"? It's their job to make things go up, just like an elevator.

15. Always do your homework before you buy so you can put a realistic value on the bundled goods and services. That's the best way to protect yourself from attractive packages that distract attention from the real cost.

16. Separate bundles of goods and services. Bid on only those that interest you. You can often get services from specialists at a lower cost or do them yourself with a little training.

17. Shop at the right place. Different vendors offer different packages of goods and services because they make different assumptions about customers' needs. By shopping at the store that offers a package best suited to your needs, you save yourself the hassle of unbundling the package.

The Baker's Dozen

Buying and selling are at the core of business activity. Used with discretion, the strategies and tactics set out in this chapter will help you become more effective in both roles. With practice, they will become second nature to you, and you will be surprised by the number of times you can use them.

We have one last idea to share with you: Whether you are buying or selling, you can always sweeten the deal for the other party after agreement has been reached. Just like a savvy baker throwing in an extra doughnut or two, you can strengthen the relationship by giving more than you need to. That's where the phrase "baker's dozen" comes from and you can use the same strategy.

YOUR MOVE

You are planning to make a real estate investment and have spent several months studying the market. One day while you are driving through a target neighborhood, you see a small office building with a weathered sign, "For Sale by Owner." The building is ideal in many respects, and you arrange to meet the owner, a retired schoolteacher. She tells you that she hasn't received a reasonable offer in the last eighteen months. As you talk, you find out why she is frustrated: Her idea of a reasonable price is 50 percent over the going market value. What can you do to get the price down to a realistic level?

You are making a regular call on an established customer. You have reviewed her inventory and usage patterns, and expect an easy sale. Unexpectedly, she says, "You know, I've always been a good customer, but I think your prices are out of line. Eric Skopec was here last week, and he says he can beat your quotation by 7 percent." What do you do?

You are negotiating a rather large sale with an established customer and have resolved most of the important issues. Things are winding down when she says, "I really appreciate your time and I like your proposal. However, I just can't see making that large a commitment without my boss's approval." What do you do?

Things are going smoothly while you review a standing order with an established customer. After a long pause, he comments, "Your deliveries are slower than anyone else I deal with. If you can't get up to speed, I may have to look elsewhere." Now what?

ANALYSIS

This is a great case to study because it involves all of the factors we have discussed. The situation is difficult because the building has been on the market for a while and the owner remains inflexible— thus, there is no real pressure to sell—and the owner is a poor judge of fair market value. Emotional attachments, personal reasons, and other people's influence have pushed the price above realistic levels.

This is going to be a tough deal, and we might walk away if we weren't convinced that we really wanted the building. However, we might try any of the following:

- Have another person make a low-ball offer. We don't rate your chances of success high, but you may readjust the owner's sense of value without offending her yourself.
- Withdraw for a while. Explain that you really like the building and appreciate the chance to see it, but you can't afford the price. Then call back every few weeks to see if there is any sign of movement.
- Test her flexibility by suggesting terms and conditions. For example, see if she will carry the mortgage and make the price or interest rate contingent on future rents.
- Try to convince her that her expectations are out of line. Bring along comparative prices, and show her what comparable buildings in the neighborhood have sold for. You have a big selling job to do if you opt for this strategy, so be prepared to take some time. And, remember, there is always a danger that someone else will make a slightly better offer, and all your hard work will benefit him instead of you.
- Build a relationship with the seller. Get to know her personally over several months. Find out what is driving her desire to sell the building, as well as the factors that she values. Be prepared to spend a lot of time listening and even helping out. If you are lucky, she will decide that she'd rather sell the building to you than anyone else.

We think the final option is your best choice. It is time-consuming, but if you really want the building, it gives you your best chance.

This is a tough case because you've been caught off guard. Don't react by criticizing your competitor. Instead, take this as an opportunity to learn more about the competition. Find out what the competition has offered and how it compares to your own package. You may be able to match the price, or you may find that your offer is still the best because you add services missing from the other.

This looks as if you have been sucker punched. Your customer has used one of the oldest tricks in the book, an appeal to higher authority. You could have avoided this by making sure your customer had needed authority, but it's too late for that now. You may be able to save the deal by dividing your proposal into smaller units, each of which falls within your customer's purchasing limits. If not, check Chapter 5 for specific means of countering higher authority.

You are in danger of losing a long-term customer. Don't get defensive. Instead, find out as much as you can about the delivery problems, and tackle the problem in two ways: Guarantee timely delivery, if you have the authority, and take your report back to the home office and see what changes can be made to ensure timely delivery.

8

Negotiating Improved Relationships

This chapter differs from others in the book because it focuses on a specific element of the negotiation process. In Chapter 1, we noted that you should always consider three factors in setting your objectives: the substantive issues, your relationship to the other side, and time constraints. All of the other chapters combine the three to give you a unified view of negotiation skills, plays, and contests. In this chapter, we single out one of the three elements: relationships.

Your relationship with the other side has a significant effect on the outcome of any negotiation. A good, trusting relationship with the other player makes it easier to share your needs and wants, and the other side will be free to do the same. This increases chances of reaching win-win agreements and paves the way for further negotiations. Conversely, a poor, hostile, or competitive relationship makes it harder to talk about what really matters to you, increases the amount of posturing and misdirection by both sides, and leads to less attractive outcomes.

Additionally, your relationship with the other party limits the kinds of strategies and tactics you may use. Short-term strategies and tactics designed to give you the upper hand are inconsistent with a good relationship. They may work once in a while because they are unexpected; however, they do lasting damage to the relationship. The other side will not be so trusting the next time, and you face the prospect of significantly less pleasant negotiations in the future.

Finally, most people deal with relationships the same way that fish react to water. Because we are constantly surrounded by relationships, we hardly notice them. People tend to concentrate on relationships only when they want to capitalize on them or realize that something has gone wrong. In contrast, savvy negotiators constantly monitor their relationships and look for ways to improve them.

As you study this chapter, you will notice that we include a lot of material that is seldom covered in negotiation books. More than any other chapter, this one is informed by our studies of communication, and for good reason. Communication scholars engage in substantial research to explore the effects of communication on relationships, and vice versa. We've adapted their most relevant findings to help you develop and maintain productive relationships. Our point of view is that of the blue-chip negotiator: Relationships are too important to take a back seat to other concerns.

This chapter will help you:

1. Identify the professional relationship that are important to you.
2. Understand why relationships require negotiation.
3. Pinpoint the features that require attention.
4. Plan and conduct a relationship negotiation.
5. Apply some specialized techniques to negotiating relationships.

Vital Professional Relationships

Relationships are the stuff of life. Researchers from many fields have demonstrated that the quality of a person's life is directly related to the number and quality of his or her personal relationships. The same is true of our professional lives.

Day in and day out, our professional lives are affected by our dealings with other people. Positive and supportive contacts enliven our work. Negative or hostile contacts can be a drag, putting a damper on our energy and enthusiasm.

Most professionals relate to clusters of people known by their titles. This cluster consists of key contacts and typically includes many of the following:

- Immediate supervisors
- Senior managers, including the boss's boss
- Immediate subordinates
- Other subordinate members of the work group
- Peers, including those in other work groups
- Key technical people in other work groups
- Customers and clients
- Members of customers' and clients' organizations
- Professional colleagues and associates at other companies

- Members of professional societies
- Old friends and mentors
- Agents and supervisors at key regulatory bodies
- Technical experts, including academic researchers and independent consultants

Each of these categories could be subdivided, and the list would continue growing if we included all of the possibilities. However, the relationships that are critical to you probably include people in each of these categories. When you have time, see if you can identify people in each of these categories that are important to you. Keep working and thinking until you have at least five in each group.

"Be kind to everyone; they might end up being your boss someday."

Maxine Kiely

Here is the key point: Each of us depends on relationships with a variety of professionals. In fact, some research suggests that accomplished professionals maintain relationships with well over 5,000 people in these categories. Your list may not be that long, but expanding it is a worthwhile goal. Properly cultivated relationships form a web or network providing you with timely information, valuable advice, and moral support. We emphasize "properly cultivated" because relationships don't just happen. They are the result of conscious, continued effort on your part.

Negotiation: A Path for Managing Relational Stress

Since we are all enmeshed in a web of relationships, you might wonder why negotiation is necessary. The answer calls for some insight into the ways relationships are formed and developed.

From the moment people are thrown together by chance or circumstance, they begin making judgments about one another. These judgments form the basis of relationships, and researchers have shown that three elements are especially important during the initial phase of a relationship: physical attractiveness, resulting from a person's physical attributes; social attractiveness, referring to a person's ability to interact with others in an agreeable manner; and, particularly important professionally, task attractiveness, which arises from a person's ability and willingness to help others accomplish their goals and objectives.

Task attractiveness is often difficult to evaluate during initial interactions, and judgments may change dramatically during the course of a relationship. In addition, problems coordinating work with the other person and external circumstances may place new demands on a relationship. Each of these events puts stress on the relationship. Research shows that people manage relational stress in three ways:

1. *Avoiding the person or the topics straining the relationship.* This way works fine when the relationship doesn't matter, because it usually leads to the end of the relationship. Ultimately disinterest or tension caused by avoidance is too much to handle, and the relationship dies a natural death.
2. *Accepting the relationship.* One or both parties know that the relationship isn't perfect but choose to maintain it without pushing for change. This is the most common strategy, and it works well for peripheral relationships, ones that don't matter a great deal.
3. *Dealing with the relationship directly.* We call this negotiation. It is the best strategy when the relationship is, or could be, important, and you are willing to invest the time and energy needed to change it in productive ways.

Picking Your Target

It helps to be as specific as possible when thinking about and negotiating relationships. Drawing on recent research, we have identified six dimensions that are important. Collectively, they add up to a good working relationship, but each can run afoul and each can be negotiated independently. Here are the six key elements:

1. *Breadth of the relationship*—the range of topics participants freely discuss with each other.
2. *Depth of the relationship*—the extent to which you disclose your feelings to the other person.
3. *Common understanding of specific tasks*—the basis for how well you work together on run-of-the-mill activities.
4. *Affection or hostility*—how positively or negatively you feel about the other person.

5. *Intensity of feeling*—how strongly you feel about the other person.
6. *Relative status*—whether you are equals or superior and subordinate.

 ## GOOD TO KNOW

Every organization has an informal organization based on personal relationships among its members. Current research points to the existence of three separate informal organizations, or networks, in every company: a *trust network,* based on relationships that involve sharing sensitive information; an *advice network,* which provides assistance in getting work done; and a *communication network,* used for sharing information about task-related matters. Significantly, managers who are central to one network may be peripheral or uninvolved in another. For additional information, see David Krackhardt and Jeffrey R. Hansen, "Informal Networks: The Company Behind the Chart," *Harvard Business Review* (July–August 1993): 103–111.

Each of these elements is vital to your working relationships. As you think about important relationships, you should be able to identify the elements that are satisfactory and those you might like to change in each. Once you have identified the element or elements you would like to change, recall a few examples of behavior in each area. Make your examples as specific as possible, but be sure to focus on behavior, not personality. Following are examples in each area, we've written them just as you might present them to someone with whom you are negotiating:

Breadth of the relationship:

"We discussed the Johnson project last week. You summarized a number of factors for me, but you didn't tell me that your new engineer wasn't trained on the CAD/CAM system."

"We did a lot of career planning during your last appraisal interview, but you never mentioned your wife's reservations about your recent promotion."

Depth of the relationship:	"We've worked together for nearly six years, but you have never told me how you feel about our partnership."
	"I appreciate your keeping me informed about your progress on the Ramirez project. Now I think we should begin talking about what you plan to do when it's finished."
Common understanding of specific tasks:	"In recent weeks, we have had some problems in coordination. We've both been trying to supervise maintenance, but neither of us has ordered spare parts."
	"I made a call on Susan Johnson at Allied last week and was surprised to learn that you had been there the day before."
Affection or hostility:	"We're working under pressure, and I'm concerned about some of your reactions. For example, last week you seemed angry when I dropped off the blueprints for stage 4 of the Carlson project."
	"I've been having some difficulty reading your moods lately. Last week, you seemed glad that we had time to review the budget, but yesterday you said I was interfering in your work."
Intensity of feeling:	"You've told me that you enjoy keeping an eye on the budget, but I don't know how strongly you feel about it."
	"Hiring decisions are critical to the division's welfare. I know you don't like me looking over your shoulder, but I had no idea it was such a sensitive issue until you shouted at me last week."

Relative status: "We work well together most of the
                     time, but last week I felt as if you were
                     giving me orders. I was particularly
                     bothered on Thursday when you told
                     me to get the report out immediately."

                     "I respect your judgment and appreci-
                     ate your input. However, there are
                     times when we simply can't stop to
                     discuss my plans. I didn't want to get
                     into a debate yesterday when I asked
                     you to review the accounts receivable."

This advance planning will help you decide whether you want
to conduct a relationship negotiation and what issue to address.
Listing specific examples helps in two ways. First, if they seem petty,
you may want to check your own perceptions before conducting the
interview. Second, focusing on specific behaviors will help the other
player concentrate on things they can change and minimize the
chances of a defensive reaction.

Conducting the Relationship Negotiation

Conducting a relationship negotiation calls for special sensitivity.
Wait until the other person is free to talk and invite her for a cup of
coffee. Pick a private place where you can talk without being over-
heard. We like to avoid offices and conference rooms because the
formality may inhibit open conversations. Restaurants and coffee
shops are among our favorite spots if they are sufficiently private,
and we have even been known to take an associate for a walk in the
park when we needed a private but informal spot.

Coincidentally, we find it difficult to schedule a relationship
negotiation in advance. Telling the other player that you "want to
discuss our relationship" may sound threatening, but simply saying,
"I need to see you next week," may leave her uncertain and anxious.

The REPA format used in other negotiations works well here too:

1. *Relate.* When you are settled in a private spot, thank her for
taking time with you and explain that you enjoy working with her,
perhaps mentioning specific aspects of the relationship that are
working well. Don't take too long with this phase because she will

probably wonder what's up, and you don't want to generate needless anxiety.

2. *Explore.* Identify your concern, and present an example or two of the behavior you would like to address. Model your statement of the problem on the examples that we provided. Now—and this may be the hardest part—wait for the other side to react. You can use questions and probes to explore her thoughts and feelings, but don't try to take charge. Building a good relationship is a cooperative process, and the other player needs to be an active participant. There is a good chance that you will learn important things about her view of the relationship, and these should be factored into any proposal.

3. *Propose.* When you are sure you understand the other player's view, and she understands yours, propose a working agreement that will preserve the vital features of the relationship while moving toward resolution of the critical issue. For example, balancing a subordinate's desire to participate in critical decisions with your need to have instructions followed is often very difficult. You might propose something like this:

> "I know that it is important for you to participate in decisions, and I realize that it is sometimes difficult to tell whether I have time to discuss an issue. Let's try this: When I'm not free to discuss something with you, I'll use the key word *urgent*. Then you will know that it has to be done without discussion. If you aren't certain, you can ask, 'Is this urgent?' What do you think of this approach?"

Closing your proposal with a question signals flexibility and opens the way for discussion.

4. *Agree.* Modify and amend your proposal as necessary to reach agreement. Plan to meet again to review the solution and make changes as needed. Here is how we would close a typical relationship negotiation:

> "Thanks for meeting with me. I value our relationship and appreciate your willingness to work with me. Let's meet at the end of the month to make sure this works as well as we expect."

Closing on a positive note will strengthen your relationship and make it easy to get back to work together.

Some Specialized Techniques for Negotiating Relationships

Because relationships are critical, some specialized techniques have been developed for negotiating them. The three that we explore here apply to a variety of situations.

Leading With Your Behavior

One of the strongest ways of building a relationship doesn't even call for discussion. Research consistently demonstrates that supportiveness is a valued commodity. You can capitalize on this insight by adapting your behavior to support a person with whom you would like to build a relationship. Three sets of behavior are critical, and each can be manipulated to demonstrate support:

1. *Loyalty,* or standing by the other person, both literally and figuratively. It doesn't call for blind acceptance of everything the other person does. Even the best of us make mistakes, and loyalty requires supporting the other person even when he errs. The key is supporting him as a person, even when he makes mistakes.
2. *Reinforcement,* or doing and saying things that will help her feel good about herself. Slavish praise wins few friends, but genuine, sincere recognition is always appreciated and constitutes a vital form of support.
3. *Support,* or helping the other person achieve her goals. Asking, "What can I do to help?" is the starting point. Following through on the commitment is essential.

Supporting your boss and other key executives calls for one other specialized tactic. Senior executives typically make a number of presentations. Their priorities and expectations are spelled out in each of these presentations, but many are frustrated by subordinates' failure to get the message. The next time you attend a briefing, don't just sit there. Take notes and watch for critical references to the speaker's needs, interests, expectations, priorities, and values.

The Job Expectancy Technique

The job expectancy technique (JET) was developed to train and develop subordinates, but you can use it whenever you have to coordinate your activities with another person. It is especially useful to the third element of relationships: developing a common understanding of specific topics.

Whenever two people have to work together, we have both of them make two lists, one consisting of their own tasks and responsibilities and the second covering the tasks and responsibilities of the other person. Both players should make their lists as complete and specific as possible. When they are done, they compare the lists and resolve any differences. Coincidentally, even people who have worked together for some time find areas of uncertainty. Sometimes both think they are individually responsible for a particular task, and sometimes neither has accepted responsibility for a key task.

By the end of the first step, both players should have complete lists of their own tasks and responsibilities, as well as those of the other player. When the lists are in complete agreement, both players take their lists aside and set priorities. Number 1 is a top priority and must be completed before anything else; 2 is next in order and must be completed before 3; and so forth.

When both players have established priorities, they compare their lists and reach agreement on the relative priorities for all tasks and responsibilities. When the tasks and responsibilities have been prioritized, both players work independently again to determine expected levels of initiative and independence. Here is a convenient coding scheme, with 6 as the highest level:

6   The task is to be completed by the person to whom it is assigned, without his or her reporting to the other player.

5   The task is to be completed by the person to whom assigned. The person reports to the other at a regularly scheduled meeting.

4   The task is to be completed by the person to whom assigned. The person reports immediately to the other player, so that the person can intervene if action will cause a problem.

3   The task requires a shared decision. The person to whom the task is assigned will recommend action but not act until both agree.

2   The task requires a shared decision. The person to whom the task is assigned will ask the other player what to do.

1   The task requires a shared decision. The person to whom it is assigned will wait to receive specific directions from the other player.

After both players have established levels of initiative and independence, they again compare lists to reach agreement. The objective is to ensure a common understanding. This final meeting should culminate in a comprehensive master list establishing tasks and responsibilities for both players, the priority for each task and responsibility, and the level of initiative and independence both will exercise.

We have used this technique in a variety of situations. Here are some adaptations you may find helpful:

- When players are superior and subordinate, list only the subordinate's activities. Over time, the subordinate's list of tasks and responsibilities should grow and move to progressively higher levels of initiative and independence. The JET may be initiated by either the superior or the subordinate. It should complement, not replace, periodic performance reviews.

GOOD TO KNOW

Building strong relationships at work does much more than make people feel good. Recent research indicates that good relationships increase employees' desire to continue working for the company, willingness to put in extra effort, and acceptance of the organization's goals and values. Relationships with top management are the most important factor, and relationships with immediate supervisors are a close second. Relationships with coworkers are less important and occasionally weaken organizational commitment. This research is reviewed by Myria Watkins Allen, "Communication and Organizational Commitment: Perceived Organizational Support as a Mediating Factor," *Communication Quarterly* 40 (Fall 1992): 357–367.

- Two people working together on a single project should focus on tasks and responsibilities that are specific to the project. This focus eliminates distractions and allows a more detailed list of project-specific activities.
- The JET may be adapted to team-building activities by posting a sheet for each team member and having other team members rotate, adding tasks and responsibilities, suggesting priorities,

and recommending levels of initiative and independence. At the end of each round, team members summarize comments on their sheets and report to the group as a whole.
- The JET may be used to coordinate activities with customers and clients. This is especially useful when engaged in long, complex projects. Periodic reviews help to keep both sides reading from the same script.

These applications are merely the tip of the iceberg. Clients constantly surprise us with new and innovative uses. Experiment with the technique whenever you need to coordinate your activities with those of one or more other people.

Treating the Other Player as a Customer

A great deal has been written about managing internal customers. You can take advantage of this thinking and research by treating everyone with whom you want to build a relationship as a customer. Here are some things you can do to demonstrate your goodwill:

- Initiate communication; don't wait for them to call you.
- Whenever they run into a problem, recommend solutions. Don't waste your time justifying old approaches.
- Be candid when communicating with them. They will appreciate your honesty and the implied trust.
- Whenever possible, communicate in person or on the telephone. Keep formal correspondence and memos to a minimum.
- Suggest ways you can improve the service they receive. Don't wait for them to request assistance.
- Use "we" problem-solving language instead of impersonal "you" phrases.
- Anticipate and solve problems before they request your help.
- Create a system to respond to their requests in a routine, businesslike manner. Avoid "fire drill" or emergency responses.
- When something goes wrong, accept responsibility. Don't try to shift blame.
- Check perceptions by asking, "Am I doing this right?" Don't wait for them to complain.
- Keep them informed while you are working on projects for them. Don't make them ask or keep them in the dark.

YOUR MOVE

You have a good relationship with a key subordinate. You have always trusted her and been open and candid in your conversations with her. Now you have learned through the grapevine that she is complaining about you and criticizing your decisions behind your back. How do you approach the situation?

You share a rather small, poorly furnished office with a coworker. You will both get private offices in eight weeks when the company moves to larger quarters, but you have an immediate problem: There is only one work table in the office. Whenever he is under pressure, your office mate moves your things from the table so he can use it. You understand his need to use the space but are troubled by the fact that he never puts your things back when he is finished. What do you do?

 ## ANALYSIS

As a starting point, you should have two concerns. First, you need to protect your sources. You will compromise your own networks if you identify the person who told you. Second, you need to find out if the rumor is true. Remember, your informant may have an agenda of his own. We suggest an informal meeting with the subordinate, leading with an open question—perhaps, "How are things going?" Skillful probing should get the subordinate to talk about anything that's bothering her. Eventually, you may want to broach the subject of her behavior, but always give the other person the benefit of a doubt. Merely expressing your concern without pointing fingers should be sufficient. If the behavior continues, you need to decide if it's serious enough to warrant disciplinary action, but we don't need to cross that bridge yet.

This is typical of the small but annoying problems people confront in organizations every day. Since you will have a private office soon, the easiest solution is to do nothing. The problem will solve itself when you move. However, you also have an opportunity to improve your relationship with your office mate by focusing on your own behavior. We wonder why you have left your things on the work table when you aren't using it. Our suggestion: Take the lead by removing your materials when you aren't using the table.

9

Negotiation Within Organizations

Thousands of negotiations take place within organizations every day. Some have dramatic consequences for everyone in the company. Examples that come to mind involve restructuring, budgeting, and strategic planning. Other negotiations affect the professional well-being of a few people—policy changes, project assignments, and hiring freezes. Finally, some negotiations are very personal—promotions and raises, educational support, and layoffs.

All of these are vitally important negotiations. Whether they affect everyone in the company, a handful of employees, or just a single person, they call for highly refined negotiation skills. The skills, techniques, and approaches you have already learned will serve you well in these situations.

Negotiations within an organization call for special sensitivity, because you will have to deal with the same people again and again. More than in any other context, earlier negotiations affect current ones, and current ones create a context that will affect the way you are treated in subsequent negotiations. Even when you are negotiating with a new member of the organization, you can expect that person to know your reputation and adjust strategies and tactics accordingly.

The need to maintain working relationships with other players limits the kinds of tactics you may use. Tricks that give you a short-term advantage will haunt you later, while efforts to promote win-win agreements will be rewarded in time. It also means that you need to be sensitive to the balance of substantive issues, relationships, transaction costs, and time pressures.

When we ask our clients what kind of help they want, many point to internal negotiations. Some raise purely personal concerns, others point to professional issues, and some list items that are hard to characterize. Here are some of the items they mention:

- Getting a raise or promotion
- Dealing with a difficult subordinate
- Dealing with an uncooperative coworker or boss
- Getting additional resources for a project
- Participating in a budget meeting
- Securing exemption from a policy or procedure
- Negotiating a cherished assignment
- Getting support to attend a seminar, meeting, or course

These are important negotiations, and they call for use of the strategies, tactics, and skills you have already learned. This chapter could focus on any of these opportunities, but recent events suggest a more specific focus.

Today, the need to cope with highly competitive environments is the dominant concern of most organizations. Survival has forced them to learn to do more with less. This is the driving force for organizations ranging from industrial giants, IBM and General Motors, to neighborhood grocery stores. It affects virtually every commercial organization between the extremes, and even not-for-profit organizations are feeling the pinch. The result is a fast-paced, challenging environment in which your negotiating skills may be tested every day. To help you cope with this environment, we will show you how to use your negotiation skills in four specialized situations:

1. Getting support from colleagues
2. Managing organizational change
3. Getting additional resources, including a raise
4. Negotiating a smooth termination

OBJECT LESSON

After several years working in the Engineering Division of her company, a bright young woman was asked to take charge of a new sales organization. She accepted eagerly, but her enthusiasm quickly turned to frustration. Her requests for support personnel, office space, and even computers were routinely rejected by the vice president of support services, who had little interest in the new organization. After eighteen months, she quit to start a new career at another company.

The lesson: Make sure you have the necessary support when you accept a challenging new assignment.

Getting Support From Colleagues

Adapting an innovative structure is one of the most common ways of doing more with less. Common examples include project management, matrix management, and concurrent engineering. Marketing and sales organizations have adopted brand or product management. Service firms increasingly use case managers to coordinate activities affecting particular clients. And virtually all organizations, commercial and not-for-profit alike, have experimented with project or action teams.

These innovations go by different names and have been developed in different settings, but the thinking behind them has two common elements. First, people with special talents and abilities are scattered throughout organizations. They spend their days working on routine tasks within their own areas, but from time to time, their talents are needed for projects outside their departments. When that happens, they may be called together for a special project or task force assignment, with a team leader appointed to coordinate their activities.

The second element is related to the first but leads to more permanent structures. Most organizations are divided into departments or groups performing specific functions—for example, sales, marketing, research and development, operations, and finance or accounting. This kind of organization promotes efficiency, and it facilitates control. At the same time—and this is one of the paradoxes of modern organizations—activities that produce value for customers cross departmental boundaries and require coordinating functional activities. For example, all five departments might be involved in a single transaction: Sales makes contact with the customer and writes the order; Marketing handles special promotions and may supervise frequent buyer discounts; Research and Development adapts prod-

---

"Being a project leader was one of the most unusual experiences in my professional career. In one way, it's like being a general manager because you are responsible for absolutely everything. At the same time, it can be enormously frustrating because you don't have any real authority. You have to get people to want to do what you say because you can't force them to do anything."

A junior executive reflecting on her experience as a project leader

---

ucts or services to meet the customer's particular needs; Operations produces the product and arranges delivery; and Finance or Accounting invoices the customer and records payments. Because all five departments are involved, there are lots of opportunities to drop the ball. Brand or product managers and case managers coordinate the activities.

Team arrangements help organizations to coordinate their resources, but they create special problems for participants and leaders alike. Three features cause particular difficulties:

1. Conflict is inevitable in these situations. Each member of the team is responsible not only to the group but to his or her home department and functional manager as well. This means that there are conflicting demands for each person's time and attention, and reward systems may not recognize individual contributions to cross-disciplinary activities. Moreover, each member has a particular specialty and may see the project differently. Each has individual priorities and preferences and a personal view of success. And each may employ a technical vocabulary or jargon that is meaningless to the others.

2. All members of the team or group must rely on people over whom they have little direct control. Each reports to a different functional manager, with common management usually several steps above the group. Going up the chain is frowned upon and may be taken as an admission of failure.

3. The unconventional nature of project teams and cross-functional management may cause skepticism among team members and

 GOOD TO KNOW

When you are leading a cross-functional team, it's important to know what motivates the members, what they value, and what they expect from you. A recent poll of new-product development teams at seventy-seven Fortune 500 organizations provides some valuable insight. Conducted by Kuczmarski and Associates, a Chicago consulting firm, the study found that a sense of accomplishment is the most important motivator, followed by peer recognition, visibility to top management, career advancement, compensation, and peer pressure. Being a doer is the most important characteristic of an effective leader.

From *Wall Street Journal* (August 18, 1993): B1.

surrounding managers. Requests for resources may be screened more closely than usual, and artificial hurdles may be created by outside managers who are seeking to maintain control.

As you can readily imagine, these features make special demands on everyone involved. Here are twelve tips that will help you negotiate your way through these situations:

1. *Build relationships with the other players* before *you need their support*. Your ability to influence them will be reduced if you show up only when you need help. Use the techniques set out in Chapter 8.

2. *Work to establish common goals.* Early in the project, pull everyone together to explore common needs and interests, as well as the needs of the organization as a whole. You can even formalize the project by crafting a mission statement that clearly identifies the principal goal and supporting elements. When in doubt, ask, "What is in the best interests of our customer?"

3. *Clarify everyone's responsibility.* Loose ends may come back to haunt you. Eliminate potential sources of disagreement by making sure everyone knows what's expected of him or her at the start. You may even do a preliminary walk-through, anticipating each step of the project and specifying responsibilities for each player.

4. *Create objective standards of performance.* Your standards should include technical elements of the project as well as how people interact with one another and the way decisions will be made.

5. *Gain the support of senior management at every stage of the project.* Getting their sign-off on the mission statement and on periodic progress reports will help to avoid problems down the line.

6. *Throughout the project, get input from everyone.* Participation will help to establish common goals and procedures, and it will generate a level of commitment that can't come from any other source.

7. *Aim to resolve conflicts through win-win negotiation.* Even minor decisions can lead to difficulty later if one or two members of the team don't think their interests are reflected. Crafting win-win agreements takes more time than other ways of

resolving inevitable conflicts, but they help to ensure continuing support and participation.

8. *Speak the language of the participants.* You can do a lot to bridge the different orientations of the participants by using an appropriate technical vocabulary at every step in the process. You may even find it necessary to translate for people with different technical specialties, but the effort will be repaid by higher levels of agreement and support.

9. *Take time to figure out what motivates each member of the team.* Some value praise and recognition, others appreciate financial rewards, and many are driven by a need to accomplish. Recognizing these differences will help you resolve conflicts and promote high levels of involvement.

10. *Publicize the group's activities.* Use memos, oral reports, and newsletters to inform everyone affected by the project. Other members of the organization may contribute ideas and expertise, and everyone will appreciate being included.

11. *Be a team player.* You can help members of the group resolve conflicts by supporting them in areas unrelated to your project.

12. *Don't play favorites.* One or two members of the group may be particularly supportive, and you should recognize their assistance. However, playing favorites can alienate other members of the team, reducing their support and sowing the seeds of dissension.

With time and experience, these suggestions will become second nature to you. When you are recognized for your ability to work with and lead groups, your career will blossom, and you will get increasing numbers of choice assignments.

Managing Organizational Change

Organizations attempting to do more with less have also introduced programs designed to change their operations. Performance management programs were popular a decade ago, and today's initiatives include total quality management, employee empowerment, and reengineering.

Some applications of these programs have been extraordinarily successful, leading to major turnarounds and rescuing organizations from the brink of bankruptcy. Other applications have had only modest success, accomplishing a little and doing little or no harm. Sadly, many applications have failed, occasionally leading to layoffs and insolvency.

Why do some programs succeed while others fail? We believe there are two factors: the appropriateness of the change program and the support of people called on to implement it.

Program Appropriateness

If a change program is an inappropriate response to the competitive environment, it cannot succeed, no matter how well it is supported. And even an appropriate change will accomplish little if it is not fully supported. Exhibit 9-1 summarizes our experiences with change programs.

Determining whether a change program is an appropriate response is a matter of strategy. We use the model in Exhibit 9-2 to help clients focus on the key elements of any business strategy: your customer's needs, your competitors' shortcomings, and your organization's capabilities. Viable business opportunities exist where the three circles overlap. Although there are conditions and qualifiers, a change is appropriate when it increases your organization's capabilities to do work that your customers value. It's even better when your competitors can't match your increased capability.

A full discussion of business strategy is beyond the scope of this

Exhibit 9-1.   Organizational change programs.

	Appropriate Response	Inappropriate Response
Well Supported	The change program will be a dramatic success.	The change program is likely to be a costly failure.
Not Well Supported	The best you can expect is limited success and uneven results. Solid results may be attained when influential managers buy in, but efforts will be compromised by the overall lack of support.	The change program is likely to break even. People may offer lip-service, but business will be conducted as usual. In other words, "no harm, no foul."

🔱 GOOD TO KNOW

There are many valuable works on business strategy. These are our favorites:

Kenichi Ohmae, *The Mind of the Strategist* (New York: McGraw-Hill, 1982).

Michael Porter, *Competitive Advantage* (New York: Free Press, 1985).

Michel Robert, *Strategy Pure and Simple* (New York: McGraw-Hill, 1993).

Eileen C. Shapiro, *How Corporate Truths Become Competitive Traps* (New York: John Wiley & Sons, 1991).

Benjamin B. Tregoe, et al., *Vision in Action* (New York: Simon and Schuster, 1989).

book, but we've listed some of our favorite sources in a Good to Know section. Our focus here is on ways you can use negotiation skills to promote change and create strong support.

Gaining Support

Promoting change is a complex process, but the basic principles are well known. Some of the more significant are summarized in a Good to Know section for your review. Negotiating agreement is important even when a change program is properly managed, and your negotiation skills are especially critical when errors have been made early in the process. In our experience, it's useful to divide people from whom you seek support for the change into five categories, tailoring your strategy to each one.

Exhibit 9-2.　Key elements of business strategy.

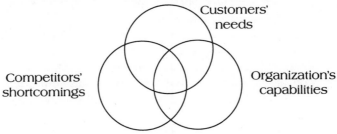

1. *The Energetic Supporter.* At first glance, you might not think you need to do much negotiation with those who vigorously support your proposal. Your natural inclination is to say, "Thank you," and turn him loose. However, his vigor and enthusiasm is also a potential liability. Unless he is managed carefully, he may criticize less active supporters, creating anger and hostility, and he may take over for weaker players, depriving them of the opportunity to participate.

When these problems emerge, meet with the energetic supporter in private. Begin by expressing your appreciation for his support. Emphasize the importance of the change and point out the importance of getting everyone on board. Then, gently, point out problems his behavior has caused. Be direct and specific, but avoid judgments and loaded words. Simply calling attention to the problem is usually sufficient. When he has acknowledged the problem, work with him to find ways to keep the project on track without offending others. Agree to keep in touch. You might even schedule several meetings, and set specific goals for his behavior.

 **GOOD TO KNOW**

Principles of Managing Change

- Create a sense of urgency by focusing on problems. Everyone needs to acknowledge that it is time for change and you can't "wait for things to get back to normal."
- Communicate a clear vision of the future. Describe it in clear and specific terms to give everyone a target and ensure that the whole organization is heading in the right direction.
- Create appropriate conditions for change by supporting and rewarding the participants while they learn new approaches, activities, and expectations.
- Involve everyone in the process. Participation minimizes resistance and gives them an opportunity to put their knowledge and experience to work.
- Open up to new opportunities, and encourage people to search out barriers to change. They may see things you don't, and you can capitalize on their insights.
- Motivate by example. Your behavior signals your true intentions; even people who don't listen will observe your conduct.
- Manage the change process over time. Identify concrete steps, create a timetable, and monitor performance.

2. *The Fair-Weather Friend.* Fair-weather friends pose a special problem. You know who we are referring to: They generally support the parts of the proposal that benefit them while criticizing other features. They may also withdraw their support when the going gets rough.

Meet with this person in private, and begin by expressing appreciation for her support. You may also emphasize your relationship by mentioning favorable results of other projects you have shared. Move quickly to the issue about which you are concerned. Avoid loaded words and judgments, and describe your concern in concrete, factual teams—for example:

> "Jane, I appreciate your support on this proposal, but I was surprised when you told Ms. Johnson that you weren't sure that it was a good idea."

Explain your concern, and then pause to let her explain her position. There may be features of which you weren't aware, and you need to let her express herself fully. When she has explained, ask, "What should we do now?" and let the discussion go where it will. When there are several ideas on the table, agree to the most favorable proposal, and make plans to keep in touch with the other person. With luck, she will emerge as a full supporter, but you also need to keep an eye on her because you can't be sure of her at critical moments.

3. *The Potential Loser.* Dramatic changes have negative consequences for some people. They may lose power, status, authority, control, or something else they value. If you don't address their concerns, they may work against you, and there is a danger of "politicizing" the proposed change.

In order to avoid problems down the line, work with the potential loser *before* heavily promoting the change. We emphasize *before* because you should find a way to accommodate him while the proposal is still in its formative stages. If you wait until the proposal has been formalized, there may be no middle ground, and the only result will be a win-lose battle. Even worse, the opportunity for change may be lost. We have seen several organizations that badly needed to change but couldn't because of the hard feelings created by earlier efforts.

As your proposal begins to take shape, mentally identify everyone who stands to lose if it is implemented. Meet with each person, one at a time, to explain your proposal, what you believe it will

accomplish, and why this is the appropriate time to implement it.
Then explain what you think the effect will be. Give the person time
to reflect on the proposal and generate a list of concerns. Use your
questioning and probing skills to help the person identify as many
concerns as possible. You need to be particularly careful here to avoid
making judgments or disagreeing. You want to hear each person out
completely to make sure there are no surprises down the road.

Once you have a complete list of concerns, it's time to begin
creative problem solving. The fact that you have taken time to consult
with and listen to the potential losers will help to limit reactions and
may stave off a destructive public debate. Minor modifications in the
proposal may satisfy their concerns. You may also need to engage in
some horse-trading, offering incentives to get each person to go
along. Sometimes public recognition is enough to gain support, and
the fact that this person is willing to go along in spite of personal
losses is a powerful argument to gather support from others.

4. *The Passive Objector.* People who play the role of passive or
"conscientious" objector respond to change proposals by saying
something like, "It's all right with me if we have to do it; just don't
expect me to support it." This is a particularly dangerous group
because while they are saying, "I'll do what I have to but no more,"
they may be biding time while planning a counterattack. At the very
least, their passive resistance will signal others that it's okay not to
go along.

We believe you are best advised to try to smoke these people out
of their holes. Meet with them individually or in small groups to
explain the proposal and why it is important. Then explain that
everyone has to be on board, and list the specific things each person
must do. Point out that the change won't do any good if a few people
go along and others wait for things to blow over.

With that background on the table, pause to hear any specific
objections. Treat anyone who speaks up as a potential loser or an
outspoken opponent. If no one voices particular objections, press for
agreement to do the work listed. The meeting is not a success unless
the objectors have voiced their objections or agreed to the specific
behaviors listed.

5. *The Outspoken Objector.* Whereas passive objectors tend to
hide, vigorous objectors lay their cards on the table. They let you
know that they are opposed to the change and voice their objections.
The greatest danger is that an outspoken objector may speak up at
the least opportune moment: in a meeting with your boss or another
senior executive, at a meeting with a customer or union representa-

tive, or in a public forum, such as a letter to the editor of your local paper. She may even become a continuing annoyance by griping about the change after critical decisions have been made and implemented.

You have to admire the outspoken objector; at least she is not hiding from you, waiting to sabotage the project. Moreover, there may be merit to her objections, and it's good for you to hear a dissenting opinion while the program is in its formative stages. We like to deal with them early in the change process, although they may generate new complaints over time.

Here is the best way to deal with outspoken objectors. In private, if possible, or in public, get her to talk about the proposal in detail. You want to make sure she understands it fully, and dispel any objections based on misunderstanding. Then draw out her concerns. Use your attending, listening, and probing skills to get as complete a list as possible. See what supports her objections. Has she seen similar programs fail? When? Where? How? Is the program inconsistent with her personal or professional goals? In what way? Does she have ethical concerns? What are they?

Your objective in drawing out the concerns is to put the complete package on the table. You should be able to see how strongly she feels about each objection and the amount of evidence supporting her position. If her objections are well founded, plan to modify the proposal. When they are not well founded, it's time to win the debate. Respond to each objection using all of the evidence at your disposal. Remember that you are making a statement that will probably become part of the public record, even if the conversation is intended to be private. The strength and quality of your reasons will determine how others respond to the proposal and the credence given to the objector's position.

Once you have won the debate, press the objector for agreement. She may never be fully supportive, but she should be willing to go along based on the evidence supporting the proposal. Eventually, you may need to push it down her throat, figuratively we hope, but you should be willing to reconsider your proposal. If there are significant numbers of vocal objectors in spite of your best reasoning and argument, it may be wise to give up. The proposal is unlikely to garner the support needed for successful implementation.

Getting Additional Resources

Few negotiations are as sensitive as those conducted when you need to ask your boss for additional resources. Here are some of the common cases in which you need to go to your boss for added support:

- You've worked long and hard and believe you are entitled to a raise.
- You plan to further your education by getting an advanced degree and would like to be reimbursed for tuition, books, and fees. You may also need to modify your work schedule to facilitate class attendance.
- A special training program is offered by a local university. Participation in the program will qualify you for certification, enhancing your ability to serve clients and customers.
- A project requires resources beyond those normally available to you. You may need expanded office space, access to a special conference room, special technical support from another division or an outside consultant, or additional equipment.
- You need exemption from a company policy. For example, your unit is shorthanded and you will be unable to complete a vital project without hiring a new employee in spite of a hiring freeze, or you are preparing to hire a particularly skilled employee but she has already received another offer for more than current pay scales allow you to offer.
- The company has a purchasing arrangement with a local vendor, but that company cannot satisfy your needs. An unapproved vendor has what you need in stock and can deliver it immediately. You need authorization to buy from the unapproved vendor.

⊛ OBJECT LESSON

With his company downsizing and reducing layers of management, one of our clients found that his opportunities to move up were blocked. With his boss's permission, he began talking with senior executives in other divisions and within a few weeks was offered a lateral move. After a little research, he found that the road to the top in that division was also blocked, and he declined the offer. Shortly after, he accepted a position in a third division that was short staffed and he has been moving up rapidly ever since.

The lesson: Lateral moves are not necessarily bad, but do your homework before you make a decision.

This appears to be a diverse list, but all of the situations have one element in common: They give rise to critical negotiations with your boss. The amount of support you need depends on the situation and your company's culture, but most modern organizations require you to go to your boss with these requests. Sometimes she has the authority to grant your request, and sometimes she must screen your request before passing it along to someone else who has the authority to grant it. In still other cases, she can grant part of your request while passing along other portions to the person who has the necessary authority.

Whatever the case, the current emphasis on doing more with less has made the process of getting additional resources more complicated than in the past. The days of automatic salary increases are long past, at least in most commercial organizations. Efforts to increase shareholder value have cut costs to the bone, and budgets have been so trimmed that resources are stretched to the limit. As a result, requests that would have been routinely approved just a few years ago are now subject to careful scrutiny.

Nevertheless, you need to fulfill your responsibilities. Even the most talented professionals need the tools of their trade. Your boss's perception is vitally important. You don't want to become known as someone who is constantly asking for more—more salary, more education, more support—but you can't afford to let your performance suffer because you don't have the tools you need. Financial problems sap your effectiveness just as do inadequate training or education, shortages of key personnel or equipment, and failure to keep abreast of current developments.

This situation gives rise to a peculiar balancing act. You need to maintain a high level of performance while constantly looking for ways to cut back. Don't expect your boss's sympathy. Odds are good that she is doing the same balancing act. In fact, it probably hit her before it hit you.

Surviving in this environment calls for refined negotiation skills and places special emphasis on your ability to find win-win solutions to tough problems (win-win because you can't afford to compromise your relationship with your boss). Consider this: Getting a substantial raise is of little value to you if the manner in which you request it puts you on the boss's hit list for the next staff reduction. The same is true of all the other requests you may make.

These are such delicate situations that students and clients have sought special assistance. Here is some of the advice they have found most valuable:

■ *Cultivate your relationship with the boss long before you need her support.* The relationship is critical because many of your requests come from her budget, and she may need to take resources from other projects to satisfy your request. The better your relationship is, the better is your chance of getting what you're requesting. Trust based on your relationship will minimize the scrutiny to which your requests are subject. Moreover, even if the resources don't come from her, she may have to go to bat for you to get resources elsewhere. Her willingness to fight for you depends on the quality of your relationship. Make sure you've committed to heart the special strategies for building relationships at the end of Chapter 8. In fact, the whole chapter will help you gain insight into the nature of professional relationships and may suggest ways of building the relationship so you can draw on it when necessary.

■ *Think about your relationships with other members of the team.* Building your relationship with your boss calls for being seen as a team player. There may well be times you need to give up resources to support other people, and occasionally losing helps to promote your image. Being a willing contributor and helping to satisfy others' special requests make your life easier because there is less chance that they will object when "she does you a favor."

Building relationships is important for another reason as well. Creating a persuasive case to support your request requires substantial knowledge about your organization. You need to know the overall priorities, under what circumstances people have been exempted from particular policies, who is looking over your boss's shoulder and what they value, what your boss's priorities are, what fires she is fighting, who may have resources that could be used to satisfy your request, and what kinds of appeals have been successful in the recent past. Learning all this calls for some artful snooping. You are more likely to get the information you need, and less likely to call unwanted attention to yourself, if you have a well-developed network based on relationships with your boss and other critical members of the organization.

■ *Lay the groundwork for your requests well in advance.* Your boss and other key executives are more likely to say yes when they have the technical background to evaluate your request appropriately. That means that you should make it a point to educate those around you in areas that will help them evaluate your requests. Here are four typical examples:

1. If you plan to request a raise soon, make sure your boss is familiar with current salary levels in your organization and elsewhere, and the procedure for granting raises.
2. Keep the boss up to date on your projects. Make sure she knows the objectives, how you are coping with the obstacles, the progress you are making, and your special needs. Encourage her to conduct regular performance appraisals. You may even introduce her to the job expectancy technique described in Chapter 8.
3. If your work requires state-of-the-art equipment, make sure your boss is familiar with models, capabilities, and vendors. You may not need new equipment immediately, but a working knowledge of the technology will help her evaluate your requests when they come and increase your chances of a favorable reply.
4. If your work requires well-trained technicians, make sure your boss knows the certification requirements, training programs that are available and the strengths and weaknesses of each, and the track record of their graduates. Don't overdo it here, but your boss's familiarity with these items will make it easier for her to say yes when one of your staff wants additional training and when you feel the need for further education.

• *Make a personal investment in getting the things you need.* Most executives will look at your behavior as an indicator of your sincerity. Taking the lead in getting resources will demonstrate your good intentions. Here are three examples:

1. A young executive knew he needed to keep abreast of current developments in reengineering. He couldn't afford to attend a commercial conference out of pocket so made a point of attending several society meetings in his area and a low-cost academic gathering. When he later applied for support to attend an expensive national meeting, it was clear that he had the necessary background, and his request was approved.
2. A young woman interested in getting an M.B.A. completed all of the in-house training programs her company offered in addition to several short courses offered by a local university. She gathered information about local M.B.A. programs and was prepared to answer all of the questions her supervisor asked when she requested reimbursement for tuition and

fees. Her request sailed through three levels of management, and she ultimately got more support than requested.

3. Struggling to finish a major project ahead of schedule, the lead engineer put in long hours. There is nothing unusual about that, but he used the time in a unique way—testing work simplification routines. Senior management was convinced that he was "working smarter" and authorized him to hire a new assistant in spite of a hiring freeze.

- *Know the real costs and values of the support you request.* We've said it before, and we will probably say it again: Doing your homework is absolutely critical. Your boss may be inclined to grant your requests without question, but she knows that others are looking over her shoulder. By doing your homework, you will be able to anticipate the questions she will be asked and provide her the information she needs to justify your request.

- *Generate persuasive reasons supporting your request.* Remembering whom you must persuade is the critical factor here. To be persuasive, your reasons need to be related to the company's goals and objectives as interpreted by your boss, her boss, and other key executives. All too often, we have seen people do an extraordinary amount of work developing the wrong sorts of reasons. What you want or deserve, what is customary, and what your associates elsewhere have isn't persuasive. Instead, you need to focus on how granting your request will contribute to the welfare of the company. Here are four examples that will help you focus on the concerns of the people who evaluate your requests:

1. To argue for a raise, demonstrate your value to the company. Show that there is a high demand for your services, you do excellent work, and replacing you would be difficult and costly.
2. To justify attending a conference, identify the specific customers and clients, real or potential, whom you will have an opportunity to court there.
3. To generate support for education and training, focus on the skills you will acquire and how they will improve service for your customers, internal and external.
4. To justify additional equipment, point out how it will contribute to the timeliness, quality, and marketability of your products and services.

- *Use leverage.* You are not going to threaten, cajole, or intimidate your boss, but knowing where you stand gives you confidence and elevates the significance of your needs and interests. Your leverage is greatest when you have accomplished something vital to the welfare of the company: winning national recognition, signing a major customer, saving a threatened account, solving a long-standing problem, or something else. Other sources of leverage include knowledge, contacts with critical customers and vendors, and a record of success.

- *Be creative when you prepare your request.* Consider alternate ways of accomplishing your objective, and give your boss some choices. Since your objective is to conduct a win-win negotiation, let her choose an approach that will cause the fewest difficulties while filling your needs. Here are five examples that should suggest a range of alternatives:

1. Alternatives to raise: Free day care, a company car, increased insurance and other benefits, flex-time scheduling, shorter hours, or an office site closer to home.
2. Alternatives to formal education: Certificate programs, in-house seminars, correspondence courses, tapes, books, and video conferences.
3. Alternatives to attending a conference: Membership in local professional societies, journal subscriptions, research assistance, and conference transcripts.
4. Alternatives to increased staff: Hiring temporary workers, university interns, reduced reporting requirements, support staff borrowed from other units, and shifting preparation of routine reports to another person.
5. Alternatives to purchasing additional equipment: Leasing, borrowing surplus equipment in other divisions, and reduced testing requirements.

You may not find all these alternatives appropriate or attractive, but they do suggest ways of meeting your needs without putting your boss in a hole.

- *Time your request carefully.* Catch your boss at the wrong moment, and she is likely to say no just to avoid a lengthy discussion. Getting her to reverse the answer later is more difficult than starting fresh, so be sure you pick a time when she can give your request the attention it deserves. Obviously, you should avoid periods of pressure, feverish activity, stress, and tension. Other times to avoid like the plague include unfavorable performance reviews, after either of you has been chewed out by someone in authority, and following announcement of unfavorable economic news. Your chances of getting a yes answer rise when your boss is in good spirits. Here are ten opportunities you may look for:

1. You have just completed a major project, on time and under budget.
2. You have just been recognzed for a major accomplishment.
3. She has just completed a major project.
4. She has just won a corporate battle and is flushed with success.
5. You have just concluded a very favorable performance review.
6. She has asked you to accept a new project or responsibility.
7. The company as a whole has just completed a winning season.
8. The business climate has made a turn for the better.
9. New products are being released with general acclaim.
10. The company or division has just won a legal or other victory.

This list, far from comprehensive, suggests the times when you have the best chance of getting what you want.

▪ *Pick an appropriate location for the negotiation.* Privacy is a principal concern. The presence of other people invites posturing and may inhibit finding a win-win solution. The boss's office is the most businesslike and ensures ready access to budget reports, company policies, and other documents that may need to be consulted. Using the boss's office also makes it easier to do the necessary paperwork while your agreement is fresh in her mind.

For all its advantages, however, the boss's office is also her turf and may put you at a disadvantage, especially if you are nervous or uncertain. Many people prefer neutral ground like a restaurant. Just remember that people get jaded quickly if you invite them out only when you have a request. Some of our clients have reported good luck negotiating with their boss at social events. They say the boss is more likely to say yes because it gives her an opportunity to demonstrate her power and authority. If you elect to try this tactic, do so with caution. Your boss may feel uncomfortable getting put on the spot, and we see this as an invitation to disaster.

▪ *Watch out for self-defeating behaviors* while you are making your request. Anxiety will signal itself in nonverbal behaviors that say, "I don't really deserve this." Your chances are even worse if you begin with tentative phrases like, "This may not be a good time, but . . ." You can avoid these knockouts by planning your introductory remarks with care. We like to be direct, something like, "I want your approval for _____. I need it because _____," filling in the blanks with a brief description of what you want and appropriate reasons for the action. Once your boss responds, don't be afraid to argue your case. It's time to stop once she says no or otherwise indicates that the case is closed. Use your own judgment; some people say no before thinking, and you may be able to push a bit. But once the decision is made, accept it and get back to work.

■ *Prepare yourself for the possible answers.* If your boss says yes, make sure you know what you need to do to implement the approval. Then say "Thank you!" and be on your way. If she says maybe, find out when you should check back, what else you can provide her to justify the request, and how you can help her find the needed resources. And, if she says no, remember that there are times when you have to accept her decision. However, you can use questions and probes to find out why she is denying your request. The more specific the response is, the more you can do to tailor your request to her needs the next time. And if she has specific reservations, find out what you can do to overcome them before making another request.

■ *Make good on your promises when your requests are fulfilled.* This is the most important point of all. Remember, increased resources bring increased expectations. You are creating a personal history. All of your future requests will be viewed in a context created by the way you use what you've already been given. Positive results—those that benefit the company—create a context in which future requests are more likely to be granted. There is also a downside: If you don't show results, the hurdles will get higher for all subsequent requests.

Negotiating a Smooth Termination

We hate to close a chapter on a sour note. However, recent events make it clear that you someday may need to negotiate a smooth termination. Here's what we suggest: Don't read the rest of this chapter if your job is secure. Know that our best advice is here, ready when you need it. For now, move on to happier thoughts.

The last few years have not been kind to the U.S. workforce. Countless thousands have lost jobs: senior executives with forty years of experience along with entry-level employees. Euphemisms abound to describe what has happened: layoffs, realignments, plant closings, workforce reductions, downsizing, and rightsizing. These phrases are evidence of discomfort with what's happening and they shouldn't disguise the reality: These people have been terminated.

"Big corporations have been whacking away big time over the past few weeks. Sears has cut 50,000 jobs, IBM has lopped off another 25,000, Boeing announced a 20,000 cut, United Technologies called for 10,500 new firings, McDonnell Douglas announced another 8,700, and Eastman Kodak fired 2,000."

Kenneth Labich, "The New Unemployed," *Fortune* (March 8, 1992): 40.

Even if you haven't lost a job, you should be alert to the possibility. A recent survey found that 43 percent of the employers contacted are reducing their workforce. The average expected cutback is just over 10 percent, but some plan cuts on the order of 40 percent. Lifetime employment is a thing of the past, and most professionals can expect to be in the market at least once a decade.

No matter how final the termination notice appears, the infamous pink slip is not the end of your relationship, and it is the starting point for negotiation. Your relationship with your former employer continues through your friends, colleagues, and professional contacts. You might even be invited back as a consultant, and your professional reputation remains in the hands of your former employer. And the negotiation has just begun.

Negotiating a smooth termination involves two steps: preparing

---

"When if first happened, losing my job at age forty-two seemed like the end of the world. I knew things were tight, but it never occurred to me that my name might be on the list. It took a while to get over the shock, but things started to come together when I calmed down. Now, I look back on losing my job as the best thing that could have happened. I'm running my own business, and I've never been happier. Everything I learned in twenty-four years working for someone else is working for me, and I like knowing that what I earn in a day is mine, all mine."

A small-business owner who made a successful transition from corporate America

---

for the termination interview and conducting yourself during the interview.

Preparing for the Termination Interview

Your termination interview may be your last formal contact with your employer, at least for a while. It can be a traumatic experience, and careful preparation is vital. Follow these steps to prepare:

1. *Accept the fact that your job is gone.* The loss of a job is a real shock, and most people need time to grieve. However, it's important to move quickly to get on with the next step in your life. Counselors can help you deal with your feelings, and you should get help immediately if you need it. You have to have your wits about you to prepare for and participate in the termination interview and to search for your next job.

2. *Review your original employment documents.* The job offer, your letter of acceptance, a contract, a letter of agreement, and any amendments may contain provisions that will help your cause. Carefully negotiated when you took the job, these agreements may be all but forgotten at termination time. While you are at it, review the employee handbook—the one in force when you were hired, as well as the current one. You never know what you will find, but it's worth looking.

3. *Find out what you can get as part of the termination package.* The company's first offer is seldom the best offer, and a quick scan of the possibilities will help you focus on what's important. Consider which of the following items may be appropriate to your severance package:

- Severance pay
- Continued medical and disability benefits
- Outplacement assistance
- Education or retraining benefits
- Favorable recommendations, including an explanation for the termination
- A job with an affiliate, partner, or other division
- An opportunity to buy your company car on favorable terms
- Continued use of your office and support systems (mailing address, telephone, fax machine, secretarial support)
- Right to buy on favorable terms surplus equipment (computers, printers, addressing machines, and other items)

- Financial planning assistance
- Bonus plan continuation
- Club membership continuation
- Accelerated vesting of stock options
- Support in developing a personal business
- Relocation assistance
- Pay for unused vacation and sick leave time
- Continuation of expense accounts and charge card privileges
- A defined consulting relationship

With regard to severance pay, one week's pay for each year of service with a minimum of two or three months is commonplace. It's often possible to do better—two or three weeks for each year of service. Also, the form of payment may be important—a lump sum if you have immediate plans, or payment over time, which may secure continued benefits, if your future is uncertain.

4. Once you know what you might get, *decide what you want.* References, training, and relocation assistance may be most useful early in your career. The right to buy surplus equipment at favorable rates and a defined consulting relationship can help you build your own business. Additional pay, financial planning assistance, vesting of stock options, and bonus plan participation may be more valuable if you are nearing planned retirement.

5. *Assess your leverage.* You may feel powerless, but you actually have quite a few points of leverage. Most companies value their reputations, and your conduct following termination is of considerable interest to them. Sources of leverage include disclosure of information that is not legally protected, relationships with key customers and suppliers, relationships with key executives and other continuing employees, relationships with regulatory officials, relationships with union representatives, and public statements about the termination and the company's conduct. When all else fails, consider the possibility of a lawsuit. We are not fond of legal proceedings, but when there may be grounds, an attorney is your best source of information. It may cost a company $100,000 or more to defend itself, and that can give you a lot of negotiating room.

6. *Take time to review your career.* How long have you been with the company? What have you contributed during that time? What are your major accomplishments? You will need to assemble this information when you begin searching for a new job, and it may come in handy during the termination interview.

Conducting Yourself During the Interview

A termination interview is unpleasant for people on both sides of the table. There's a lot at stake, and you need to play your cards right. Remember that this is an adversarial situation, even if it's conducted by an old friend. The person conducting the interview will probably be cordial and professional. Expect him to try to make you comfortable, but never forget that this is a win-lose negotiation. Anything you don't ask for stays in the company's pocket. With that in mind, follow these guidelines:

- *Take careful notes during the interview and use a checklist to make sure all your interests are addressed and all your questions are answered.* You can seldom go back for more once you've signed a final release.
- *Create a context for the negotiation by summarizing your years of service and major accomplishments.* They may not sway the other person, but reciting them will help keep them in mind and bolster your feelings of self-worth.
- *Be frank about your needs.* Explain what kinds of support you need and why. Don't be reluctant to talk about your children's college tuition, your mortgage, the tight job market, and your sick mother. You may not convince the other person, but the list will help keep the interview focused on what's important to you.
- *Do not whine, complain, or criticize either the company or the executive handling the termination.* Your fussing can't restore your job; however, it can damage your reputation after the fact and stampede your boss into a vindictive decision if you push too hard in the wrong direction.
- *Do not accept a premature settlement.* It isn't easy to reopen a signed termination agreement, and it's better to leave it unsigned until you are satisfied. If the other person presses you to sign, take a break. Walk away, relax, and reschedule the interview. His pressure may signal weakness in his position. Take time to consider the offer and explore other alternatives.

★ YOUR MOVE

In recent months, your company has received a growing number of complaints from customers about slow and unpredictable delivery.

Worse, Customer Service representatives are often unable to help because the delayed orders have not been entered into the Customer Service database. Reviewing the order fulfillment process, you find that orders placed by the sales force are routed to Accounting for credit checks before they are forwarded to Customer Service, Manufacturing, or Distribution. You believe you could improve customer service by having a copy of the order sent to Customer Service at the same time the order is sent to Accounting. The order would not be packaged or delivered without approval from Accounting, but the Customer Service representatives would be able to tell customers what was happening to the order when they called.

You have explained your proposal to the other senior managers, and almost everyone likes your proposal. However, the senior vice president of Accounting has flatly refused to consider it and will use all her authority and influence to block the change. What do you do?

You have recently been hired to manage the accounting department of a small firm. You report to the vice president of Administration, but your responsibilities include preparing reports for several other vice presidents, especially of operations and marketing.

When you took the job, you noted that your staff badly needed cross-training. Each did his or her own job without helping the others. As a result, one or two people were always overwhelmed, while others sat back and took it easy. Worse, when one was out of the office for any reason, his or her work just piled up. Important tasks came to a halt for as long as four weeks when one of the senior clerks went on vacation.

You realized that cross-training would temporarily delay some routine reports while your staff learned new tasks, but neither you nor the vice president of Administration thought it would be a major obstacle. Just to make sure, you sent an explanatory memo to other vice presidents and department heads to explain the cross-training process and your reasons for implementing it.

Things have been going well, but this morning the operations vice president called you into his office. "What the hell is going on? Why can't I get answers to my questions? I need the information now, not when your clerks get done with this silly exercise!" Shaken because you didn't know how to deal with this situation, you returned to your office and pulled a clerk from training to complete the required report. That solved the immediate problem, but the whole cross-training program is in jeopardy. Now what?

 ANALYSIS

This is a difficult situation because a key executive has refused to consider your proposal. Your first step should be finding out why. If she won't discuss the matter with you, use your network to see what you can learn. There are several possibilities: She is locked in a power struggle with someone else and sees your proposal as an additional threat, she has seen similar proposals fail in the past, she fears loss of power and influence, critical members of her staff oppose the change, and so forth. The point is, you won't know how to proceed until you find out why she is so strongly opposed. Once you understand her opposition, you will be able to find an alternate approach.

Coincidentally, her fears of losing power and influence may be well grounded. Some companies have found that so few customers default on payments that credit checks are unnecessary. They have actually saved money by eliminating credit checks and the needed staff, improving delivery times, and accepting the loss on a few uncollectible invoices.

Although your boss approved the project, she doesn't seem willing to come to your aid, and her decision is the right one. You don't want this issue to trigger a turf fight between the two vice presidents. The first rule of organizational survival is never to be responsible for such a squabble.

Let's reconstruct what may have happened. The operations vice president either didn't read your memo or didn't realize how it would affect him. Make a note to avoid this problem in the future by meeting directly with influential people who will be affected by changes you institute.

While we're at it, it's good to note that you did the right thing in getting the report to the operations vice president rather than throwing the memo in his face. Tempting as it might be, this would only set up a confrontation that you can't win.

To salvage the situation, treat the operations vice president as a potential loser. With your boss's consent, schedule a private meeting to explain what you are trying to accomplish and how it will benefit everyone. Give him time to identify potential problems and begin generating solutions. Modify or amend your cross-training program, if necessary, and publicly thank him for his support.

Don't forget the other vice presidents. So far only one has had a problem, but that might be an early warning sign. Meet with each of the others to make sure they understand your project, identifying potential problems and developing potential solutions before you find yourself on the hot seat again.

10

Playing Referee: The Role of the Mediator

As you master the skills and approaches described in earlier chapters, your colleagues will notice your ability to negotiate win-win and other agreements, and they will begin calling on you to help them negotiate. When that happens, you have entered into a whole new game, playing mediator, with unique moves, countermoves, and challenging situations. To help you make the transition, this chapter will:

1. Tell you when to mediate and when to refuse
2. Help you set realistic expectations
3. Identify the special contributions you can make
4. Summarize the mediation process

When to Punt and When to Play

The first time they are asked to mediate, most people are so complimented that their enthusiasm overrides their judgment. Before long, they find themselves caught in a morass of conflicting emotions, charges and countercharges, and moves and countermoves. By the time they realize what's happened, they are trapped; it's too late to

---

"Mediation is negotiation assisted by a third party."

W. L. Ury, J. M. Brett, and S. B. Goldberg, *Getting Disputes Resolved: Designing Systems to Cut the Costs of Conflict* (San Francisco: Jossey-Bass, 1988), p. 49.

---

withdraw, and there is no clear path ahead. At the very least, they face a period of thankless work. Often, neither of the disputants is satisfied with the results, and the mediator loses friends, stature, and sleep. Even a successful mediation is an emotional drain. A friend once described her experience by saying, "The operation was a success but it felt as if the doctor died!"

To avoid these distressing situations, watch for some red flags:

- *The negotiation has gotten acrimonious.* Both parties may be looking for a scapegoat. By becoming involved, you will be a candidate.
- *You are personally involved in issues or have a stake in the outcome.* It's almost impossible to mediate in this situation. Once your interests are known, neither disputant will trust your judgment or direction.
- *There are long-standing problems that other skilled mediators have been unable to resolve.* Probably neither of the disputants is flexible enough to reach a winning solution.
- *The disputants have or can develop the perspectives and skills to negotiate without your help.* Involving a third party delays solution. If you become involved, you merely give them an excuse to continue unacceptable behavior.

When you see one or more of these red flags, get out of the way gracefully. Simply say:

"I appreciate being asked, but I just don't think I can be neutral here."

Then recommend someone else.

Without the red flags, mediation can be a rewarding experience. Mediation is most likely to lead to positive results in the following situations:

- Both sides seem to be willing to give a little but have gotten too involved to back down. A mediator can often find alternatives that save face for both while resolving the core issues.
- The disputants are acting as agents for people who have power over them but are not actually participating. Without help, the disputants may be unable to make needed concessions. The mediator makes it possible for both sides to give a little without being blamed for failure.
- The negotiators are well intended but lack the skills to make

the process work. The guidance and coaching of a skilled mediator can compensate for their shortcomings and teach them some important techniques in the process.

- The dispute is deadlocked over minor or procedural issues. By accepting responsibility for the process, a mediator can remove the initial roadblocks and get the process back on track. Any of the deadlock breakers described in Chapter 3 can get things moving again.
- Both disputants value their relationship but are hung up on substantive issues. The critical perspective of an outsider can often reframe the dispute. Simply recognizing the significance of the issues for both sides and helping each see the other's view may open the way for innovative solutions.
- Creative thinking is required. Both disputants may be so involved defending their positions that they are unable to come up with alternatives. The need is even greater when the negotiation has gotten contentious and both disputants fear that considering alternatives will weaken their position.

Setting Realistic Expectations

Understanding what mediation is and how it is related to other forms of conflict resolution will help you set reasonable expectations.

As you have seen, *negotiation* is a form of conflict resolution in which the players try to resolve the dispute by themselves. It is characterized by give and take between the participants, neither of whom can impose their will on the other.

Arbitration is a more formal approach to conflict resolution. Both sides make their case to a third person, who decides the issues. With nonbinding arbitration, the third party can recommend solutions but cannot impose judgment. In binding arbitration, the arbitrator has the authority to impose a solution.

Our judicial system provides a third form of conflict resolution, *mediation*, which falls between the other two. In civil matters, both sides make their case following prescribed rules. The disputants represent themselves in small claims court; attorneys are the key players in higher courts. Once both sides have been heard, the judge or jury decides how the situation should be resolved, and all the resources of the judiciary are available to enforce the judgment.

As a form of dispute resolution, mediation falls between negotiation and arbitration. The mediator oversees the process and helps both sides present their cases. She often structures the process to give both sides an equal opportunity and may suggest innovative approaches when the process appears deadlocked. In extreme cases, the mediator may even side with one of the disputants, recommending resolution of one or more issues in her favor, but the mediator has no authority to impose a solution. This feature gives rise to one of the most telling characteristics of mediation: No matter how one-sided the contest, the mediator must rely on the goodwill of the disputants to reach and abide by a mutually acceptable solution.

The job of the mediator is to negotiate the procedural issues, establish the relationships among the negotiators, explore their interests, propose strategies, and secure agreement. As a result, there are some things you can do—control the process, make sure both sides have an opportunity to present their cases, make sure the participants understand one another, and adhere to the procedural rules—and some things you can't—develop an ideal solution, mandate agreement, or enforce a preferred solution. Aim too high, and you are sure to be disappointed.

The Mediator's Contributions

Mediators can neither impose a solution nor ensure that agreements are carried out but still make vital contributions to the process. Concentrating on following key contributions will ensure that your time and effort are well spent.

Facilitation

As a facilitator, you govern the process from the beginning to the end. In a typical negotiation, participants worry about both substantive and procedural issues. As a mediator, you accept responsibility for the procedural issues, freeing the participants to concentrate on the substantive issues. Most important, the mediator facilitates by establishing norms—the ground rules—for rational interaction: mutual respect, open communication, no use of coercion, and the desirability of mutual satisfaction. In mediation, the negotiators supply the content of the problem to be solved, and you should supply the process. The meeting management skills discussed in Chapter 3 are also necessary, such as setting the ground rules and occasionally paraphrasing and summarzing. It also helps to write on large flipcharts that are posted for easy reference. This helps keep the focus and yet lets you refer back to what has been said.

 **GOOD TO KNOW**

"Some of the communication tactics mediators can use:

1. Ask the parties to define terms.
2. Point out the differences in their definitions.
3. Negotiate a consensus on definitions.
4. Fractionate the conflict. In other words, label all parts separately and individually to reduce each element into a workable proportion.
5. Rearrange words in new ways.
6. Relabel terms the disputants cannot agree upon.
7. Label the nonverbal behaviors so they can be mediated.
8. Get specific answers for the questions who, what, when, where, how, how much, and what if.
9. Clarify mutual obligations.
10. Get verbal commitments.
11. Continue asking, 'How can both parties win?' "

From Laree Kiely and Dan Crary, "Effective Mediation: A Communication Approach to Consubstantiality," *Mediation Quarterly* 12 (June 1986): 47–48.

Environmental Guardian

Closely related to facilitation is creating an appropriate environment, one in which disputants can meet without distraction and without elements that might interfere with the process. The shape of the meeting table is a major concern. Rectangular tables have clearly defined dominant positions—the head and foot—and people often jockey for a particular spot. To avoid giving either side an advantage, you should occupy the dominant position, while the disputants occupy equal side positions. Table shapes can vary according to the type of case. More formal settings may be comfortable to business operators, less comfortable to consumers, more conducive to resolving disputes in ongoing close personal relationships, and most desirable in situations that can rapidly get out of control, where the setting should be used to accentuate the importance of abiding by the rules. Or, you may choose to have no table at all between the parties. This is a very open, informal setting, best used to maintain the close relationship between parties who have little need for writing, a maximum need to interact, and who both feel safe.

Translation

As a mediator, your interpretive listening skills are critical because you must restate, reword, rephrase, and reinterpret the negotiators' content. Your goal is to translate their words with more linguistic diversity than they are able to use and with more descriptive language rather than loaded words. You also have to make sure that all parties arrive at similar definitions of terms to ensure agreement on language and help define the real issues.

Creative and Critical Thinker

As the clear-headed person in a mediation, you will be expected to help find creative solutions and ways to implement them. This goal assists negotiators in discovering and then finally agreeing upon a mutually satisfying, viable solution.

There is another payoff for demonstrating this skill: It teaches others the importance of stretching outside imaginary limits for possible solutions. Your job is to add and elicit new information in order to extend the range of choices. In terms of functional cooperation among the negotiators, you can help determine possible solutions and make sure that the agreement reached is workable.

As critical thinker, your task is to stay logical and rational, look for the hidden assumptions behind the parties' statements, and attempt to discover leaps or gaps in logic and inconsistencies for the negotiators so that they can arrive at a mutually satisfying outcome.

Educator

By serving as a mediator, you can help people in the long term as well as the short term. A mediator also teaches. You instruct by giving information, but even more by modeling appropriate behavior in the form of conflict management, communication, and negotiation skills. This process has at its core the desire to keep the relationship between the disputants intact.

The Mediation Process

There are four phases to mediating:

Phase 1: Set the stage for the process. You set ground rules, explain what is going to happen, build rapport with both parties, and ask each side to articulate their perspective and the other side's perspective. You then ask why they are there and what they would like to end up with as a result of the mediation.

Phase 2: Establish the relationships between the negotiators and begin to explore the matter. Determine their individual interests and their areas of similarity and disagreement. Get as much information on the negotiating parties and the history of their dispute as possible.

Phase 3: Start exploring strategies for resolution. By now, you know most of the important information, but since new data keep coming up as you go along, don't be surprised if either side throws you a curve.

If the body of the mediation itself takes more than one meeting, the first stage of the subsequent meetings is to summarize where the previous meeting left off. Whenever possible, limit the number of meetings and the time in between to keep the negotiators from starting over every time and rehashing issues that have already been resolved.

During the process, you can caucus with the negotiators—take the parties aside and talk to them individually rather than in front of each other. Caucusing is occasionally useful when one side wants to consider alternative solutions but not appear weak or too conciliatory, tell secrets, keep from doing harm to relationships, or discuss something without the other side's hearing. It may also be useful when you want to say something to one party without the other party's hearing or don't want other party to lose face. To be a successful strategy, however, both parties must be given an equal opportunity to caucus with the mediator so they will continue to feel the trust and impartiality of the mediator.

Phase 4: Wrap up the mediation. This is where you secure agreement and check to see if the parties really are satisfied with the resolution and intend to follow through with the determined outcome. Then you summarize and the parties outline the steps toward implementation, the time line, and who is accountable. You could also ask what was learned about dispute resolution and what the parties would do differently the next time to be more effective on their own as negotiators. This is particularly important if you are the manager of these people and want them to succeed without you next time.

A clear ending to the process is important to the attitudes of the parties, their sense of completion, and their desire to implement the solution. Remember to compliment all of the players for their participation, declare the mediation a success, and adjourn.

Learning More

Mediation is a powerful tool as a backup to negotiation. It is most useful when negotiation isn't going to work and prior to escalating differences into the courts. There are many excellent books on the subject, which has been called a growth industry of the 1990s. If you need a mediator, check out the Yellow Pages, look up your local dispute resolution centers, call the Academy of Family Mediators, check with the conciliation courts, talk to the National Association of Mediation in Education, or contact the Society for Professionals in Dispute Resolution. If you want to become a professional mediator, training is available through all of these organizations.

If you want to be a more effective human being overall and know how to manage conflict and help others do the same, learn the skills and get involved.

YOUR MOVE

You're a sales manager, and two of your sales reps are disputing who gets to service a major customer that has moved from Rep A's territory to Rep B's territory. They have tried to negotiate and have reached an impasse. They ask you to resolve the dispute for them. What do you do?

ANALYSIS

First, decide if you can be neutral. If so, go back to them and tell them you won't resolve it for them, but you will mediate. Why? So you can teach them some skills and not have to be the tie breaker in the future. Make them responsible for their own fate and for keeping their relationship intact at the same time. This strategy uses all of the chapters in the book, including the one on negotiating relationships. By offering to mediate rather than decide, you have also negotiated your relationship with each of them. If that's your answer, too, good call!

Index